JENNIFER'S DIMES

BY

BARBARA L. ACKER

2018

Cover photo from IStock
Photo ID# 500156852
Credit: Ivanastar

Published by Barbara L. Acker

ISBN-13: 978-1726185677

ISBN-10: 1726185672

Dedicated to my loving husband Tim,
Who is my rock and best friend!
Without you, none of this would be possible!!

To my wonderful son who has been
There for me more times than I would like
To count! You are my "Hero"!

Finally, to the most important person of all,
my daughter Jennifer.
Thank you for the dimes and for watching out
over all of us.
I love and miss you more and more
with each passing day.

November 16, 1988 – June 14, 2011

CONTENTS

CHAPTER 1

THE START OF IT ALL

In the fall of 2007, I had pretty much hit the lowest of lows. A three-year divorce battle was taking its toll on me. I felt like a ship out at sea during a hurricane, with no rudder. Tossed, beaten, and utterly lost. Even the church that I had been born and raised in seemed to have turned its back on me. Could it be that God had abandoned me? Or even worse, forgotten about me entirely? Those were just a few of the many thoughts and feelings I was having when I received a forwarded email. Another cute story sent to me by some person who had nothing better to do with their time than forward emails, I had thought to myself at the time.

The story was about a rich man who had a friend come to visit for a weekend. One evening while the friend was there, the two of them went out to dinner. As they were making their way into the restaurant the friend observed the rich man bend over and pick up a penny that had been lying on the ground. A warm and serene expression came over the rich man's face as he held that penny in his hand. He looked at it lovingly for several seconds and then with a smile, he tucked it away into his shirt pocket. That episode remained on the friend's mind all through their dinner. Finally, once dessert was being served, she couldn't contain her curiosity any longer and asked the rich man why that simple penny seemed to mean so much to him. The rich man, in response, questioned his friend, "What does it say on the penny?" The friend shrugged her shoulders and replied, "One cent?" "No, try again," answered the rich man. "United States of America," said the friend, shaking her head in uncertainty. Once again, the reply from the rich man was "No." Finally, it slowly began to dawn on the friend, "Oh, I know," she exclaimed. "In God, we trust." "Yes," replied the rich man. "Every time I find a penny, it is a reminder to me from the Creator that I should be trusting in him, and all will be well."

I had thought to myself at the time, "What a cute story" and then deleted it like I had done in the past with all the other forwarded messages I had received. However, that one particular story was different. It kept playing over and over in my mind to the point where I actually wished I had saved it.

Wouldn't you know it, a few weeks later, there was the same story once again in my email box, sent to me by a different friend. That time, I saved it and copied the part of the rich man's answer of why the penny meant so much to him. I pasted it onto some construction paper and laminated it, so I could always have the explanation to refer to. Somehow, that simple story and its account of the significance of the penny to the rich man really resonated with me. That was the start of the lifeline that I had been so desperately searching for.

Ever since I was a young child, it had been my habit to walk as much as possible for exercise. Each day, during my lunch hour, I would walk roughly two to three miles around the neighborhood from where I worked. Funny thing was, since having read that email about the rich man and his penny, I started to find my own pennies almost every time that I went out walking. This seemed to be especially true on the days that my mind traveled to the woes of my impending divorce.

Thanksgiving time slowly rolled around, and my parents came for a visit. Being extremely devoted church goers, they were very upset about the diminishment of my faith and non-attendance at church. My mother insisted that I should attend Thanksgiving mass with them. I was really in no mood to be participating in such a service, but with a heavy sigh of resignation I finally conceded, just to make her happy. In the meantime, I had shared with my mom the penny story and how it had been slowly helping to uplift my spirit to some degree. I explained to her how I seemed to be finding pennies whenever I was worried about the divorce battle. She appeared interested but a bit unimpressed. My mother informed me that she thought it might be more sheer coincidence rather than a sign from above. However, as she wrapped me in her warm embrace, she told me that if the pennies gave me some solace, then she was all for it.

The time eventually came for us to head off to church. I was dreading having to sit through a service that my heart was just not into. I truly wished I had not agreed to go. "What had I been thinking?" Begrudgingly, I sat in the pew halfheartedly listening to the priest as he droned on with the mass. All the while, the turmoil that had been eating away at my faith washed back over me. Could it be possible that the pennies were not signs like my mother suggested but instead just pure accidental finds? Maybe the pennies meant nothing at all and I was being absolutely foolish for believing in them. My head spun with all those potentially dangerous thoughts. It was at that point that the priest got up to give his homily. He began to speak about an email that he had just recently received from a fellow parishioner. It was a story concerning a rich man and a penny! My mouth dropped open and an audible gasp escaped my lips. My mother turned and looked at me with wide eyes. What were the odds that the priest would choose that story to tell on that particular day? Was God trying to tell me something? Only time would tell.

The experience at the church began to help slowly restore my faith in what the pennies might truly mean. That surge of newfound hope helped me get through the next several months as the pressure of the divorce mounted. Court was delayed twice. Each time it brought the same doubt and fear back into my mind. Looking back, I am not sure why I had so much anxiety over all that was going on. I just knew that I felt like a tightrope walker who could fall at any moment, and there would be no safety net to catch me. My stress level was at an all-time high. I believe now, that any little thing would have made me snap back then. It was during that time, I was out for one of my daily walks. Of course, my mind was racing over the impending court date and all the ramifications that it held. The distress had begun to mount, and I was finding it hard to breathe, when suddenly I saw a penny on the road. "What a find, especially right now," I had thought to myself. I bent over to pick it up. As I did so, I heard the Holy Spirit speak to me saying, "Look at that penny... See how beaten up and almost unrecognizable it is. That is, **you** and how **you** are feeling right now. However, the bottom line is, that penny is still a penny, and you are still you. I am always going to be here for you. *So, please stop worrying.*" I held onto that penny like it was my life preserver to a rescuing ship.

Several weeks later, court got postponed a third time. I had hit my breaking point. I was hysterical and out of control. I cried for two solid hours. I questioned, when would this nightmare ever end? I was so angry at God, that in my frustration, I threw my beat-up penny, screaming at him, "You promised to be there for me!" I couldn't possibly see how this would be for the best. My whole world was turning upside down and I seemed to have no control over what was happening to me. I felt like a drowning child, flailing in the waves, waiting to possibly be rescued but instead only finding the big bully who was trying to drown me in the first place.

Several days later, while cleaning my living room, I found that thrown penny. It allowed me to take a deep breath and try to come to terms with what was happening in my life right then. I know now what I didn't know then, that all things happen for a reason and in God's time, not necessarily our own. However, sometimes, that wait between our time and the Creators can be extremely painful. I still have that penny to this day. It holds so much meaning for me. It serves as a constant reminder of a time in my life when all seemed lost and then suddenly a wonderful light broke through the darkness to give me much needed peace for a brighter day.

The date for court was set one more time. Finally, we proceeded as planned. I was a nervous wreck. What if I said or did the wrong thing. I don't think very clearly under pressure. What if they asked me questions and I couldn't give them an answer because I was too flustered? What if there were tons of people sitting there waiting to hear our dirty laundry? The good, the bad and the ugly. How embarrassing! What if the other lawyer portrayed me as someone I wasn't? Would the judge be able to see how miserable my life was with my husband and grant me the divorce? Those were just a few of the many thoughts that were racing in my head at that time. I decided to take that beat-up penny with me to court. Each time I started to feel the fear, or nervousness welling up inside me, I would caress that penny in my hand and know that I needed to put my trust in the Almighty. With him by my side, together we would get through it.

The following Saturday, after my first day in court, I woke up with my mind racing, in great distress, over what I should have said or done differently at the divorce hearing. I needed to try and clear my head, to think good and positive thoughts. It happened to be a beautiful spring day, the kind that makes you wish you were a child again with no cares in the world but what to do with such a gorgeous day. The sun was shining, and the call of the sea gulls beckoned me to the local Atlantic coastline. A place that usually offered me great comfort and delight. However, that particular day, while I walked on the beach, my mind still kept wandering to those negative concerns. I was struggling to keep the anxiety down and to think positively, when I saw a weathered warn penny sticking up between the beautiful pieces of shells, small rocks, and shimmering white sand. I picked it up with trembling fingers and clutched it to my breast. A warm and calming sensation washed over my body. I felt like I had been wrapped up in a warm blanket on a cold winters night. I was so overwhelmed with emotion of having made that discovery. What were the odds of finding a penny on a beach, right there, right then? I could only believe that it was another gentle reminder from the Lord of Peace that he was walking beside me through my valley of darkness.

The second day of the divorce hearing came, and it was just as rough as the first one. Not only was my husband there to tell terrible stories about me and our life together but he had brought our daughters to the justice building as well. I was stunned, when I walked into the court room and saw them sitting there. I immediately became sick to my stomach and I had to rush from the room before anyone could see me get sick. My lawyer followed me outside, not exactly sure what was going on. Shaking, I informed him that I was not confident I could proceed with my children sitting in the same room where our unhappy marriage was going to unfold. He explained to me that it would not look good to the judge if I left, so I had to put on my big girl pants, face my fears and stay. That would be one of the hardest things I ever had to do. Unfortunately, years later I would face an even more awful day, but for now I had to get through it. Thankfully, I had my beat-up, weathered warn penny with me, and because of it and knowing that God was with me, I was able to make it through. No one ever tells you how awful something like that can be. Your whole married life, played out for others to sit in judgment of you. If it wasn't for the fact that I knew I had to get out of my marriage *to save myself,* there is no way I could have gone through with what I went through those two days. One surely never knows how strong they can be until they are faced with the most insurmountable of odds. It is only then, that we learn what we truly are capable of.

The next day, July 29, 2008, I left with my son Joe for Texas, to visit my parents for two and half weeks. That was a much-needed vacation. It would give me some time away from all the fear and anxiety that the divorce was causing me. Plus, it was family time, which I so desperately desired. I don't care how old you are; there is nothing like a parent's hug to bring some peace and tranquility back into your life.

On August 14, 2008, I awoke to hear the whispering of the Great Spirit speaking to me. He told me that it was essential for me to share my story with others. That I needed to let people know what his love and peace had done for me and what his divine graces could do for them as well. So, once I got back to New York from Texas, I began to recount my tale of the pennies to those whom I thought would be interested in hearing what I had to say. One of the people that I spoke with was my good friend Kathy. Like me, Kathy had been going through a difficult divorce and was having a hard time dealing with all her worries. Shortly after I shared with her my account of the found pennies, she had an extremely rough week. She just couldn't seem to be able to shake off all her anxieties. She explained to me that one evening while getting ready for bed, she decided to trust me in what I had told her and offered up all her fears in prayer. Kathy informed God that she was completely handing everything over to him. No more trepidations, no more worries. She also told me that she prayed that the Great Spirit might speak to her like he had spoken to me. If only he could send her a tiny "sign" that things were going to be okay. She just needed some type of indication that she had been heard to help relieve her concerns and anxieties. The very next morning, she disclosed to me that she awoke with the thought in her head, "All will be well." Which, in itself, she proclaimed to me was a comfort that she had never felt before. However, after getting dressed and starting to head downstairs for breakfast, she felt a small piece of gravel in her shoe. She went to the kitchen table, sat down, took off her sneaker and dumped what she thought to be a pebble into her outstretched palm. To her shock and dismay the object that landed into her hand was no small rock, but a penny instead! Kathy confessed to me that at that very moment she knew that the Lord of Light had heard her prayer, and all was going to be well for her. That account only confirmed to me that I truly needed to be sharing my story so that others, like Kathy, could experience the overwhelming love and peace that our Heavenly Father has to bestow on us.

On September 20, 2008, I was scheduled to go out with my friend Kathy to buy frames at the craft store for some new pictures I had enlarged to display on my apartment walls. Unfortunately, I was in no mood to really be going anywhere. Being the human that I am, I was having a very difficult time emotionally once again. It had been a rough week for me. There had been no word on the divorce judgement. Then there was the relationship between my landlord and I which was not going well. Plus, nothing new had happened with a possible job change that I was looking to partake in. And finally, my son Joe was struggling at home with what should have been my ex-husband. Life could be so frustrating at times. I thought about calling Kathy and canceling but I knew she wouldn't let me. Besides, I really wanted to get those picture frames. So, I tried to put on a cheery face and not let my depression show. However, my dear friend saw right through me as soon as I arrived. She gave me a huge hug and told me we were going to have FUN no matter what.

Kathy and I decided that we were both really hungry and could eat something before we headed over to the craft store. So off we drove, discussing as we went, where we thought we might want to eat. I made a suggestion of a Mexican place I knew called, "The Taco Stand." Kathy agreed; that sounded good to her. Then I happened to remember I had a local coupon book in my car. Since I was driving I asked Kathy to check it and see if there were any discounts we could use for the Mexican restaurant. Instead, she found a coupon for a sports bar that was next door to "The Taco Stand," which we had heard served really good burgers. Together, we agreed we would like to give that place a try instead of the original plan of Mexican food. We arrived at the establishment and placed our orders. While we waited for our food, Kathy inquired why I was in such a funk. She reminded me how I just needed to put my trust in God, let him take care of my life and not worry so much. I had been in such a good place just a few weeks ago, she pointed out. I needed to get myself back there mentally. As much as I knew all of that, I was just having a hard time making myself believe it. With that, the waitress returned with our drinks. As she set my glass down in front of me, I shrieked and began to cry. Kathy couldn't figure out what was going on with me. "Was there something wrong with Barbara's drink," she wondered? But then I slowly turned my soda around to show her what I had seen. The image of a penny imprinted on the side of my glass! Hers had no such graphic. Also, it was only on one side of the cup: the exact side the waitress placed the drink facing me. With that, I felt the weight of the past week slip away from my body. An extreme sense of peace washed over me. That simple penny design was my sign of who was in charge and always would be in charge if I would completely let him be. I just needed to remind myself of that fact, and when I forgot, He would remind me once again. I bought that "penny" glass from the restaurant and now have it prominently displayed on my desk at home. It is one of several glasses that I now own, in which I place all of the pennies I have found since that ordeal began. So many pennies.

On Monday September 22, 2008, the decision came in from the judge in regard to my request to dissolve my marriage. He would NOT be granting the divorce. In the state of New York, at that time, "irreconcilable differences" was not allowed as a reason for a separation of a couple. If someone wanted to end their marriage, they had to prove, beyond a shadow of a doubt either mental or physical cruelty or infidelity. Apparently, the judge did not feel I had proven my case. To say I was stunned and shocked would be an understatement. I was trembling inwardly when I received the awful news from my lawyer but was able to hold it together long enough to finish my conversation with him. However, once I ended the phone call, the tears began to flow. I felt like I had been punched in the gut. My chest hurt, and it seemed like I couldn't catch my breath. I dialed my parents to give them the devastating news. It was so hard for me to understand how this could possibly be for the best. I cried for several days and struggled with the shear raw emotion of it all. Three years of fighting with what should have been my ex-husband, to what end? How did any of this make sense? Was I truly supposed to stay in a loveless relationship? I couldn't see how our Lord would have wanted that for me. What was I supposed to do now? I was so confused. What would become of me? How much more was I supposed to bear? If only I had known then what was to happen in the near future, I would never have asked that very last question.

On the following Saturday, I decided I needed to finally get out of my apartment and run some errands. Even though I was still in no mood to deal with anyone or anything, I knew I had to do something to pick myself back up and try to live whatever life it was that I was meant to be living. I arrived at the store and parked my car, not even remembering the drive there, as my mind wandered in all different directions. As I got out of my car something bright caught my eye. The way the sun was hitting it, made it shimmer and sparkle, like the light from a newly lit candle. I leaned in closer to see what it was. A brand new, extremely polished penny. As I bent to pick it up, I heard my Savior telling me that this was "ME", and that I would soon be just like that penny, all brand new and shiny. I felt the comfort of his words wrap around my body, almost like someone gave me a huge hug of understanding, and immediately I no longer felt like crying. I truly believed that what he was telling me would come to pass. Once again, I had to abide my time and wait until God was ready to show me his ultimate plan. I knew someday I would become that bright and lustrous new penny.

As life continued, I was still finding myself falling at times into my old ways of thinking. However, it never seemed to fail that whenever that happened, that was when I found more pennies. They were always there to remind me that the Lord of Peace heard my thoughts and prayers. To remind me that "He" was still in charge and would always be there helping me along life's path. God has promised me great things, and I knew through his love and grace, it would come to pass, but in "His" time, not mine. In the meantime, I had to put my trust in him and hold out for those pennies from heaven to appear.

For the next several months, as I settled into the knowledge of my situation and new spiritualism, the contentment that I felt carried over into everything. I found it amazing that I could find so many pennies when I was in need of them, and yet now that I was in a good place, and I didn't need them, none seemed to be around.

Starting around the Christmas holidays and carrying over into the New Year, I was once again allowing myself to be distracted by too many outside influences. The anxiety in my life began to build. I was very frustrated at work. I thought I was being led to do something different, but nothing seemed to be coming my way. My living situation had turned into a horrible mess. My landlord and I were no longer seeing eye to eye and she was making it very difficult for me to stay in that apartment. I needed to move. However, one move attempt in November had fallen through leaving me questioning where it was that I was supposed to be going. "What was it that I was supposed to be doing?" Then there were the approaching holidays. "Who wants to be alone for Christmas, their birthday (Dec. 26th) and or New Year's? Not me." I was expressing all this angst to my friend Kathy on Sunday, December 4th, on our way to church. She turned to me and said, "Whoa, you are going crazy. The poor universe doesn't know which thing to give to you." I realized she was right. My thoughts were all over the place. How would the Great Spirit know what to give me first if I didn't know what I wanted? I decided I needed to focus on one thing at a time in my life. First up, a new place to live.

The following Wednesday, I went to lunch with my girlfriend Donna. While at the restaurant, I went to fill up my glass with soda from the self-serve machine. What do you think I found lying on the counter next to the soda machine? Yep, you guessed it, a penny. I smiled, knowing that heaven had heard my prayer.

The next day, while I flipped through the local newspaper entitled the Pennysaver, I saw an ad for an apartment. It was in my price range, which if you know anything at all about New York and Long Island, that was not an easy thing to find. Unfortunately, it was listed as a studio apartment. I was not sure that would work for me; *however*, it did provide a washer and dryer, something most apartments do not offer. That would be really nice to have access to. No phone number was given but they asked for responses to go to an email address. Something inside me told me to send a message, and so I did. What could it hurt? The next day, I got a response back from the owner of the apartment, thanking me for my interest. However, she informed me that she had had an overwhelming response of sixty people and had already rented the place. I was surprisingly disappointed but figured it wasn't meant to be. In spite of that, I was feeling so good about what life might have in store for me that I decided to send her a reply back. I just wanted to thank her for letting me know the situation with the apartment and wished her all the best with the new tenant. The next afternoon, I was home working on some crafts when I received a phone call. It was the landlady of the place that I had looked into from the Pennysaver. She was wondering if I was still interested in the apartment. It seemed the new tenant had fallen through. The owner told me that since she thought she had rented the place she had gotten rid of all the other applicants' phone numbers and email addresses. All she had left was my thank you email which had arrived after she had deleted all the other's contact information. Wow, God really does work in mysterious ways!

JENNIFER'S DIMES

CHAPTER
2

THE IN-BETWEEN YEARS

The new apartment was great. Even though it was a studio rental, it was almost the entire basement of the owner's home. It had been completely updated and refurbished. I was able to make it into a lovely living space for myself. Plus, I had that awesome washer and dryer. You couldn't get any better than that. My new landlords were wonderful people who became even better friends over time. God really knew how to take care of me, especially when I sat back and let him run the show. With no family in the area except for my children, it was nice that I knew I had folks who were willing to watch over me and make sure that I was safe.

Once I had my amazing new living quarters, I began to work on some of the other aspects of my life that I was not so happy with. Unfortunately, the divorce thing was still dragging on. It was sucking a lot of my time and energy. New York State had finally passed a law to recognize "irreconcilable differences" as a reason for dissolving a marriage. That new statute would have allowed me to try to get another court date. However, my lawyer, not to mention my husband's attorney, were dragging their feet to get anything done. I was extremely frustrated. At that point, it was four years and counting since my ex and I had separated.

I still didn't know what I was supposed to be doing with my life. I was working as a school secretary, but some major changes had happened in my district. That upheaval caused my original position at the elementary level to become part-time; therefore, I was moved into a redesigned full-time arrangement. That new placement meant that I floated around the school district from office to office, as the demands of certain schools warranted the extra help. I enjoyed the new challenges and getting to meet different people; however, not having one set place to call my own was upsetting at the time. I was thankful that I had my part time, weekend job to go to. At least there, I was able to relax and decompress from the weekday chaos.

Shortly after my husband and I separated, I had decided to pursue a new hobby. I had always loved water activities, such as swimming and canoeing. Therefore, when I saw an ad for kayaking lessons being offered at the local gym with an indoor pool, I decided to sign up for them. It turned out that I was the only one to register for that particular class. That enabled me to get one-on-one lessons with the instructor without having to pay for such special attention.

Once I finished the classes, I wanted to put my new-found ability to use. Since I lived on Long Island at the time, I could paddle some bays or the ocean, but there really wasn't much river kayaking available. Ever since I had learned how to use a canoe as a teenager, going down rivers had always been my first choice over lakes or ponds. There was just so much more to be seen along a shoreline when you could paddle by quietly in a boat. There were many times that I had been able to approach some amazing wildlife that you wouldn't have normally been able to see otherwise.

When my daughters where younger and involved in Girl Scouts, I remembered having visited a whitewater rafting company in Pennsylvania. That outfit used river guides in kayaks to help the rafting customers go down the waterway. I thought maybe that would be a fun way for me to try out my newly acquired boating skills and get paid for doing it at the same time. Pennsylvania wasn't too far from Long Island, roughly two and half hours with no traffic. I didn't mind driving that distance if I would be doing something I truly enjoyed. Plus, it would put me back into the country atmosphere that I had grown up in as a child and loved so much.

So, one weekend in May, I drove to Pennsylvania to visit the rafting outfit to see if I would be able to get employment there. It turned out they had already hired their entire group of river guides for the new season. However, I was informed that they were still in need of help at their adventure center. I was told that if I worked there, I would still be able to train with the guides and hopefully get placed when a position opened up. I decided that was an acceptable compromise; besides I thoroughly enjoyed my time in Pennsylvania. I felt so relaxed there, and the people were super friendly. I had found a new place to call home on the weekends.

For the next few summers, I traveled back and forth every other weekend to Pennsylvania during the rafting season. I enjoyed my work at the center, and I learned about everyone who was employed there. One of those people that I was especially glad to get to know was Tim, the assistant manager. I discovered him to be a fantastic boss and a very caring person. The longer we worked together, Tim and I gradually learned that we had many similar interests, not to mention the fact that we both took great pleasure in making one another laugh. We slowly became wonderful friends, as each season passed. Tim and I found that we just truly enjoyed each other's company and I ascertained Tim to be an amazing listener. He was extremely supportive over my frustrating divorce issue. That in itself was a great comfort to me to have someone that I could talk to about it. However, at the end of each season, we remained just co-workers and lost touch with one another over the long winter breaks. As each break passed, I found myself missing Tim more and more during those extended winter months. Unbeknownst to me, Tim was feeling the same way.

Over the winter of 2009, Tim started to realize that he was having more than friendship feelings towards me. The following summer he tried to convey his fondness for me but was a bit shy and worried about being shot down. Plus, we were still co-workers and he was afraid of jeopardizing that relationship. However, I suspected things were different when he seemed to hang around talking to me more than usual. He also appeared to be worried about my welfare. If I happened to mention that I was hungry or cold, he would magically appear with some food or a jacket. It was wonderful to be noticed like that, but I was still not quite sure that he wasn't just doing those things to be nice.

My son, Joseph, had been working with me at the whitewater rafting center for the past couple summers. Tim was also his assistant manager. Apparently, Joe had seen the same changes in Tim that I had seen. When I expressed my confusion over Tim's actions to my son, he informed me, "Mom, Tim really likes you." Of course, I was pleasantly surprised to hear that news, but I was a bit confused. I asked Joe how he knew that to be true, and his response to me was, "We guys just know these things."

I was excited to learn that Tim might have feelings for me, but how did I find out for sure? As it turned out, my son's birthday fell on a day we were working at the rafting center. I decided it would be fun to have a small birthday bonfire for him at the company campground. We scheduled it for a time after we got off from work. I invited fellow co-workers and friends of Joseph's from the adventure center. Plus, it allowed me to invite Tim. My hope was that he would come, and we would spend some time together outside of the work environment. So, I had put my plan into motion, and was delighted when Tim agreed to attend.

The night of the bonfire arrived with much apprehension and excitement on my part. "What if Tim didn't show?" "What if things were awkward between us?" "What if I didn't make a good impression?" Those were just some of the many thoughts that raced through my mind that night. It was difficult for me at that time to set up for the party without my nervousness being shown. I felt like a high school girl getting ready for her first date. I never thought I would ever feel that way again.

The party started, and everyone was having a great time, but there still was no Tim. "Maybe he changed his mind?" "No, he wouldn't do that to me," I had thought at the time. "There had to be another reason." Fortunately, I wouldn't have to wait too much longer before Tim finally arrived. He apologized for his tardiness but explained that it had taken him longer to close up the camp store than he had anticipated. I was just thrilled that he had finally shown up at all.

Tim presented my son with a baseball cap for his favorite ball team. Joe thanked him for the gift and then ran back to be with his friends around the campfire. Luckily, my son and his companions were happy to keep themselves entertained at the party. That enabled Tim and me to be able to spend the evening talking and laughing like never before. So much for all my fears. We seemed to have so much in common that it was almost freaky. I felt so comfortable around Tim that I was able to share with him some of my "Penny Stories". He seemed to be impressed by them.

But more importantly, he didn't think I was crazy for believing what I thought it all meant. That was a huge relief for me.

As we were sharing stories and laughing, an innocent hand on a knee sent a bolt of emotions through both of us. I felt really good about how the evening went between us. I hoped that maybe Tim would give me a kiss good-night. But I was disappointed when Tim said he had to go and just got up and walked away. I was crushed. "Didn't Tim feel the same way about me as I did about him?" I wondered. Unbeknownst to me, Tim was extremely nervous and afraid to try for that kiss. However, several minutes later, I was pleasantly surprised when Tim re-appeared with a bottle of water for me. He had gone back to the camp store just to fetch me something to drink. Apparently, he had overheard me saying earlier how thirsty I was after we had run out of drinks at the party. "Maybe he does like me after all," I thought to myself. Since that would be my last night of the season at the rafting center, Tim did give me a quick hug good-bye before he finally left. I was comforted by the fact that we had exchanged phone numbers and also agreed to stay in touch with one another over the winter months.

A few weeks went by, but I didn't hear anything from Tim. Once again, the old self-doubts started to creep in, and I wondered if maybe I was wrong about his feelings for me. I had never dated anyone that was so shy and hesitant before. I was not sure what to do. Since I have an impatient side, I decided to take matters into my own hands and thought I would give Tim a call. However, I didn't want to appear too pushy, so I was grateful when an opportunity presented itself for me to have a reason to call him for some advice.

I arrived home one evening from work to hear a squirrel running around in the ceiling of my apartment. My landlords were away in

Florida, and I had no one else close by who might have been able to assist me. I decided that would be my golden opportunity to contact Tim to see if maybe he had any ideas on how to get rid of that stupid rodent. At least by using that excuse I felt it wouldn't seem I was being too desperate. Tim seemed pleased to hear from me, which was a great relief. However, months later, he did confide in me that he thought it was pretty funny that I had called him all the way in Pennsylvania to learn how to get a squirrel out of my ceiling in New York. "How did I think he was going to be able to help me from there?" I didn't really know, but hey, at least it was a good excuse to telephone him.

Over the next few weeks, there were many phone calls between the two of us. Conversations that lasted into the wee hours of the morning. It seemed Tim and I could talk about anything and everything. Each time we were speaking to one another, neither one of us wanted to let the other one go. That was extremely amusing, since both of us really hated being on the telephone normally. After several weeks of carrying on like that, we decided to have our first "real" date. The next opportunity for us to do that was when I came back to Pennsylvania to attend an employee barbecue. We decided that we would go out after the party was over. However, we agreed that we wouldn't let on at the gathering that we were interested in each other, just in case the dating thing did not work out for us. Neither one of us wanted it to ruin our working relationship. So, the fewer people who knew about us, the better.

The days seemed to pass so slowly, as the anticipation of seeing Tim once again, truly excited me. To make things even more complicated, my parents had decided to come for a visit, from out of state. I explained to them that while they were visiting me, we would be making a trip to Pennsylvania. Fortunately, my parents were willing to humor me and went along for the ride. We rented a hotel room close to the town where the party was being held. Since the gathering did not start until later in the afternoon that day, I took my parents sightseeing for most of the day. It was torture for me to watch the hours slowly tick by. Then finally it was time to attend the barbecue. I could hardly wait! I felt like a little kid on Christmas morning waiting to open presents from Santa.

Tim and I agreed that we would arrive separately to the gathering. That would enable us to not let on to anyone at the party that there was anything going on between the two of us. My parents and I arrived at the cook-out and began to mingle with the crowd. I couldn't help it, but I kept glancing towards the front of the house as I waited to get my first glimpse of Tim. It seemed like the minutes dragged on forever. The weather was overcast that day, and it had begun to drizzle. We were under a covered pavilion, but I informed my parents that I was going to go back to the car to get umbrellas. I wanted to have them just in case it began to rain harder when it was time for us to leave later that evening.

I walked around to the front of the house where the vehicles were parked. I was struggling with car doors and umbrellas when I heard my name being called. I turned around to see the most wonderful sight. Tim had finally arrived! Just like a perfectly planned plot of a movie, we found ourselves alone. I ran to him, and he took me into his arms and gave me the biggest bear hug I had ever received in my life! It felt so good to be in his arms and to see him after all our nightly conversations. Neither one of us seemed to notice or mind that the rain had started to come down harder than before. He finally released me from his bear hug, and I couldn't wipe the silly grin from my face. I felt like I was in another world, and I didn't want to break the spell. After we exchanged a few pleasantries, Tim walked me back to my vehicle. He helped me lock the car and assisted me in carrying the umbrellas.

Tim and I walked back to where the barbeque was being held. I introduced him to my parents. They too had been anxiously waiting to meet him ever since I told them about the real reason we had for going to Pennsylvania. They were in on our little secret as well, of not letting on too much so that others at the party wouldn't have known that anything was going on between Tim and me. I was thankful that they were willing to play along.

After Tim met my folks, he and I went our separate ways. It was so difficult to be there watching Tim and not let on about my true feelings for him. Each moment at that party was pure torture. Occasionally, I would sneak a glance in Tim's direction and I also would feel that he was doing the same. Since we did work together, and people knew we were friends, we were able to sit across from each other while we ate and conversed with everyone there. Finally, it was time to say good-bye to everybody at the party and leave in our separate vehicles. Tim waited to leave for several minutes after my parents and I did. Prior to the barbeque, I had told Tim where we would be spending the night. He and I had agreed to meet there once we had left the gathering.

My parents and I went back to our hotel room. My mother and father began to settle in for the evening while I raced to freshen up my make-up and re-do my rain-soaked hair. Once I was ready, I nervously paced back and forth in the room while I waited for Tim to arrive. I was so jumpy that I felt like a cat on a hot tin roof. Finally, there was a loud knock on the hotel room door. My heart was pounding loudly as I rushed to open the door. I prayed I wouldn't pass out from the sheer excitement of it all. I swung the door open wide to see Tim standing there looking more handsome than I could ever remember. It almost took my breath away. Such strong emotions I was feeling that night. I was not sure I had EVER felt that way before. Tim smiled at me and slowly pulled from behind his back the biggest and most beautiful bouquet of flowers I had ever seen. And then with his other hand he presented me with a box of chocolates as well. I was stunned. No one had ever done anything like that for me before. It was just like a love scene from a romantic movie. I was so lucky to have found such a wonderful and caring person.

Tim had previously asked our rafting center manager if she knew of a good place to go eat. She had recommended a country pub that she knew, which actually happened to be the same place she and her husband had their first date. So, Tim walked me to his car and opened the passenger side door for me. I thought to myself, "Wow, he was a true gentleman." We drove toward the recommended establishment where we planned to have a light meal and some drinks. The entire trip was spent just talking and laughing like so many of our past phone conversations. Once we arrived at the pub, we were in the middle of a conversation, so Tim parked the vehicle and we just continued speaking to one another. At one point, Tim asked me if I wanted to go in to the restaurant, but we were having such a nice time sharing personal stories in the car that I didn't want to break the spell by getting out and going into the establishment. Besides, it was nice to be sitting so close to him and not having any noise or interruptions like those that might have occurred in the pub. So, we decided to just stay put and talk and talk and talk. Before we knew it, *five* hours had passed, and we never made it out of the vehicle! Funny thing was, due to all of the hot air coming from our conversation, the car windows fogged over. Anyone who might have passed by would have thought we must have been making out in the car, but Tim was so shy that he hadn't even tried for a kiss yet. We had, however, at least gotten to the point where we held hands while we sat in the vehicle and shared stories from our lives. By then, it had gotten too late to go into the pub, so Tim turned the car around and drove me back to the place I was staying with my folks. He escorted me into the hotel and down the hall to the door of my rented room. Finally, he worked up enough courage to kiss me. Our first kiss! I had once asked my aunt, who had met her soul mate, how she knew he was "The One." Her reply to me was, "You will just know." Well at that very moment, with that first kiss, I finally knew what my aunt meant. I had met my *soul mate*.

A little over a year later, on March 20, 2011, with many miles on two vehicles, lots of E-ZPass dollars spent and more cell phone minutes than you could possibly imagine, Tim surprised me by proposing with the most beautiful heart shaped diamond ring while sitting on a boulder at the beach. The very beach that I had taken him to the first time he came to visit me on Long Island. Now if I could only get that divorce. It was six years and counting.

JENNIFER'S DIMES

CHAPTER 3

THE NIGHTMARE BEGINS

In May of 2011, I began to find dimes, *not* pennies. I mean lots and lots of dimes. They were everywhere. Dropped on the floor in front of a cash register; left behind on a counter in a store; next to a sink in a public bathroom; shining brightly by the side of the road during my daily walks; laying on the pavement next to the gas pump; under a chair in a restaurant; my change due back from a purchase, all in dimes (Seriously, who does that?); and so on and so on. I was finding so many dimes that I really had to question why? I thought they might possibly be a sign from Tim's dad who passed away that previous January. I asked Tim if he knew that might be the case. But he informed me, "No" he couldn't think of any reason why his father would be sending this type of a sign. Both of us were left wondering why I would be finding so many dimes and not my usual pennies. Unfortunately, the answer to that question would become all too clear that following month.

Tuesday, June 14, 2011 was like any other beautiful spring day on Long Island. I awakened to the glorious smell of flowers blooming and the sound of birds chirping outside my bedroom window. It was a wonderful sensory stimulus to wake up to. I bounded from my bed with anticipation of what the new day would hold for me. However, if I had only known how awful that day was going to turn out I would have thrown the covers over my head and never gotten out of that bed ever! But since the day was young and I had no knowledge of what lay ahead of me, I got dressed, packed up my lunch for work, and headed for the door. As I went to leave the apartment, I bent over to kiss my son Joseph good-bye. At that time, Joe was living with me until he graduated from high school and left for the Navy that following January. That day he was home from school as it was finals week at the high school, and he had no exams to take. As I walked to my car, I ran into my landlord Brian who was busy watering the front lawn. I was pleasantly surprised to see that he was home. Brian worked for a professional New York baseball team and traveled a lot for his job. We chatted for a few minutes in the front yard, and then I had to hurry to get into my car to head off to work.

I arrived at school and began to get settled into my usual daily routine. At approximately 9:45 a.m., my personal cell phone rang. I glanced at the caller ID and was surprised to see that it was my middle daughter calling. Seeing her name come across my cell phone caused me to hesitate for a moment. You see that particular child of mine had not spoken to me in over six and a half years! Not since her father and I separated, and I had filed for the divorce. "Why would she be calling me now?" I wondered. I cautiously answered the phone. My daughter asked me if I knew where her brother was. As far as I knew, he was at my apartment still sleeping. I could hear by the tone in her voice that she was very upset about something, so I asked her if everything was ok. She informed me that she just needed to speak to my son *right away*. I assured her that he was at the apartment sleeping and she should call him on his cell phone. She explained to me, however, that she had already tried that, but he didn't answer his phone. At that time, I could still perceive she was very distraught about something, so I communicated to her that I knew my landlord was home. I told her, I would be willing to telephone Brian to ask him to go down and let my son know he should call his sister right away. Once more, I asked my daughter if there was anything I could do for her, but she told me "No"; that she just really needed to speak to Joseph as soon as possible. She thanked me for my time and then I heard the click of the phone being hung up. All the while I was speaking to her, a feeling of foreboding washed over me. Call it a mother's intuition, but I sensed something was extremely wrong. My boss happened by as I hung up the phone and saw the worried look etched on my face. She asked me nonchalantly, "What's up?" I responded, "I am not sure, but something doesn't feel right." I then proceeded to telephone my landlord Brian, who thankfully answered my call. I questioned him if he was still at his house and was relieved to learn that he was. I asked if he wouldn't mind going down to my apartment and letting my son know he needed to call his middle sister right away. Again, having that sense that something might be amiss, I asked Brian if he wouldn't mind staying with my son while he made that call as I was just not sure what was going on. In the back of my mind, I was thinking that perhaps one of my estranged husband's relatives had passed away. I knew that there were a couple of them that were ill and not doing so well. Brian said "Sure" and hung up the phone. I tried to go back to work but I was troubled by the nagging sense of impending doom.

About ten minutes went by when my cell phone rang again. This time I saw from the caller ID that it was my son calling. That sense of foreboding and dread swept through my body once more. In my mind, I figured he was calling to tell me someone had died. NEVER in my wildest dreams did I imagine it would be the person whom he tells me it was. I anticipated it being his grandfather who had been in a nursing home and was very sickly. So, I quickly answered the phone and moved towards a doorway where my cell phone could get better reception. I could hear Joe crying uncontrollably on the other end of the line. I asked "Joseph, what is the matter?" All the while, I was still thinking he was going to tell me that one of his grandparents had passed away. It was very difficult to understand him as he was crying so hard. He commented that someone was dead, but I couldn't make out the name of the person that he was speaking of. I pressed him once again, "Joe, honey, who's dead?" He says, "…..is dead." I don't know if he was crying so hard that I couldn't understand him or if my brain just refused to process what it was that he was trying to tell me, so one more time I said "Joe, Who Is Dead?" Again, my son declared "Jen is dead!" At that moment, it began to slowly register in my brain and I started saying "Jen….Jen…Jennifer, MY DAUGHTER JENNIFER?" "WAS DEAD?!?" I felt like someone had just slugged me in the chest, and I couldn't catch my breath. Apparently, at that point I must have been screaming pretty loudly because my boss came running over and tried to lead me away from the doorway where students and teachers could have seen me. As fate would have it, at that very moment, the school psychologist happened to be coming into the library to take out some special books. He made sure no children were in the room and then closed the library doors. I was shaking and crying uncontrollably at that point. I was having a hard time comprehending what it was my son was trying to tell me. I immediately developed a severe headache; the room was spinning, and I felt like I was looking at everyone and everything through a thick haze. At that point, my boss Beth, had now taken the cell phone away from me and was discussing the issue with my son. She finished talking with Joseph and hung up the phone. The school psychologist had directed me to a chair and offered up a box of Kleenex's. I sat there, crying while the news settled into my brain. I just couldn't stop crying or shaking. It was at that point, Beth and the school psychologist decided it would be wise to get the building principal. Meanwhile, I was thinking, I *don't even* know how she died. Was it a car accident? Some other type of accident? What could have befallen my baby girl???

There are huge gaps in my memory from that day. I don't remember who called Tim; my parents; or my best friend Kathy. I assume it was my boss, but I truly don't know. I have tried to recollect all that happened in those minutes after receiving that awful news but all I have is a patchwork of memories. I do remember my principal came down and just stood there looking at me with a concerned expression on her face. I guess she did not know what to say or do. No one did, including me! At some point, it was decided that Beth would drive me back to my apartment in my vehicle, and one of the custodians would follow us in another car to bring my boss back to school.

The principal and the school psychologist each gave me a quick hug and expressed their sympathy for my loss. Beth and I left the school and headed out. I don't remember the car ride home, but I assume I was a big blubbering mess. I just couldn't stop crying or shaking. As we neared my apartment, we passed my landlord's car with my son in it, headed in the opposite direction. Brian was on his way to bring Joseph to my ex's house. He saw us pass his car, so he turned the vehicle around and pulled up behind us in front of his home. My son jumped out of the vehicle and ran over to me. We grabbed ahold of each other, all the while we cried like babies. Joseph and I clung to each other like our lives depended on it. We must have made quite a scene out there on the front lawn, but neither one of us cared. I don't remember, but I am pretty sure I asked Joe if he knew what had happened to his sister, but he didn't. After several minutes had passed of us clinging to one another, my landlord gently tapped me on the shoulder and said he was going to drive Joseph down to his father's house. I slowly let my son go after I kissed him good-bye and then I turned to head into my apartment. At that moment, I realized that my boss and the custodian were still awkwardly standing there by the vehicles. I walked over to them and thanked them for having brought me home. They each gave me a hug and expressed their deepest sympathies for my loss. They both had such a sad look on their faces. I couldn't even begin to imagine what I must have looked like at that point. Swollen, blood shot eyes with trails imprinted on my cheeks from the tears that had run freely down my face. They turned to get into the custodian's car and headed back to school. At that very moment, my best friend Kathy pulled up. She sprinted out of her car and ran over to me. I collapsed into her arms as I sobbed hysterically once again. Kathy knew all three of my children. She has been a dear, close friend ever since my kids were very little. She even used to babysit for me when I needed, so this was a huge loss for her as well. We stood there once again making a spectacle in the front yard. Finally, as my outpouring of agony slowed, Kathy coaxed me towards my apartment.

Once we made it inside, the confusion as to what had just happened and what I should have been doing next hit me. I felt like a sleep walker in a very heavy daze. I just stood there inside the doorway, looking around my apartment, as I tried to get my brain to work somehow. But before I could really figure out what I should be doing next, my cell phone rang. I didn't recognize the number that came up on my caller ID and I really was not in the mood to talk to anyone. However, something inside me told me I should answer it, so I did. I heard what I thought was my ex-husband's voice on the line. He sounded like how I felt. My ex informed me that he was still at the hospital. He was calling to see if I desired to come and see Jennifer before the medical examiner took her away. Without thought or hesitation, I responded, "Yes." I then asked him what had happened to our baby girl, as I still didn't know the reason for her death. Unfortunately, like my other daughter who had called earlier that day, Jennifer has not spoken to me since her father and I separated six and half years before. So as much as it pained me, I was not a part of her existence at that point and not privy to what was going on in her life. My ex-husband informed me that Jennifer had just graduated from college the weekend before, and his family had a graduation party for her on Saturday. The next morning, she had woken up complaining of not feeling well. Apparently, she slept most of that day and barely ate anything. Sometime on Monday she started to take a turn for the worse and told her father that he needed to take her to the emergency room.

When my daughter was 14 years old, she was diagnosed with a disease called Lupus. Since that time, Jen has been in and out of the hospital on occasion dealing with some of the side effects of that awful illness. Having not known what was wrong with Jennifer at the time; my ex-husband took her to the hospital where she had gone in the past for treatment. That medical facility was over a forty-five-minute drive away from where they lived, but my estranged husband felt that would be a safer bet, just in case. Unfortunately, even though my ex brought Jennifer to that better hospital it would not be good enough. Her blood platelet count was extremely low. The doctors and nurses tried multiple treatments with Jen but while she was in the emergency room she began to have problems with her breathing. She complained that her chest hurt as well. The doctors decided to intubate her to help her breathe more easily. At some point early Tuesday morning, Jennifer went into cardiac arrest. To everyone's shock and dismay, the doctors were unable to bring her back.

I listened to all that information my ex-husband was telling me, but I was having a hard time believing it all to be true. Jennifer was only 22 years old! How did she go into cardiac arrest at that age? She had her whole life ahead of her. My head was throbbing, and it was hard for me to even think clearly, but I tried desperately to focus on what he was telling me. At that point, I informed my ex that I was on my way to the hospital and would get there as quickly as I could. I hung up my cell phone and asked Kathy if she would mind driving me to the hospital. There was no way I could drive in the condition I was in. Thankfully, Kathy said "of course." So out the door we went.

It took us roughly 40 minutes to get to that hospital. I was so thankful that I had such a wonderful friend like Kathy to drive me. I was an emotional mess. My head hurt so badly, not to mention my heart. I felt like someone had stuck a knife into it and twisted with all their might. I just kept playing over and over again in my mind the phone call from my son. How was this occurring? You hear of things like this happening to others, but never do you dream that someday it could happen to you. We finally arrived at the hospital, but Kathy couldn't find a parking spot. She decided it would be best to drop me off by the emergency room doors. Once she had found a place to park, she would come in and find me. I hesitated over that decision as I really didn't want to have to walk into the hospital alone. However, I also didn't want to miss out on seeing my daughter for one last time, so I finally agreed and climbed out of the vehicle.

I entered the emergency room doors and was immediately met by a security guard. He asked me what I was there for. I felt like I was in a bad nightmare and I couldn't wake up. I struggled to inform him who I was and that I was there to see my daughter, Jennifer. At that point, a nurse who overheard the conversation came running to my side, put her arm around my waist, and ushered me down a long hallway. All the while, I felt the eyes of the entire emergency room staff upon me. I couldn't help but wonder what they must have been thinking. The nurse tried to comfort me by saying how sorry she was for my loss. But how could you possibly console a mother who had just learned she had lost her eldest child! The emergency room nurse led me to a door which read "Family Room" on it. She proceeded to open the door and there sitting on a sofa was my estranged husband, his new girlfriend, and one of my ex sisters-in-law. Immediately, my ex sister-in-law jumped up and came over to me and gave me a huge hug. For several minutes, we just stood there clinging to each other, all the while we sobbed uncontrollably. My ex-husband didn't move or even seem to acknowledge that I was there. He looked like he was completely worn out, both physically and emotionally. I marveled to myself at how old he looked and wonder if I looked the same way right then. His girlfriend, who I had seen in passing but had never officially met, got up and introduced herself to me. She expressed her deepest sympathy for my loss and then returned to sit by my ex on the sofa. I was thankful he had her with him during that most difficult time. I so desperately wished that Tim was there with me right then. Oh, how I could have used his comforting arms around me. However, it would take him at least three hours to get to New York from Pennsylvania once he was able to get on the road.

An uneasy quiet settled over us and we all just sat there, like that, for several moments. Each person was lost in their own thoughts. Finally, there was a quiet knock on the door. In walked the same nurse who had just brought me to that room. She asked if we were ready to go see Jennifer. My ex slowly rose from the sofa almost in a zombie like state. Together, he and I followed the nurse out the door and down the hallway. I kept looking around for Kathy, but to my chagrin, she was nowhere to be seen. I was thankful that my ex sister-in-law and my husband's girlfriend did not come with us. It would be just two parents with their oldest child. We proceeded down the hallway with our heavy hearts. My feet felt like I had lead in them, and it was taking incredible effort on my part to not just turn and run in the opposite direction. Maybe if I wouldn't think about it, it wouldn't be true?!? As we walked down the hospital hallway, we passed people chatting and laughing like everything was "normal," but it wasn't. I wanted to scream at them and tell them to stop laughing. Couldn't they see that my whole world had been turned upside down, and it would never be "normal" again? Life was so cruel. What did we do to deserve such heartache? I couldn't imagine that my heart would ever stop hurting. It had been broken in two, and a piece of it was gone, lost forever, along with my daughter.

My ex informed me that they had to leave Jennifer exactly the way she was when she passed. He told me the medical examiner would be doing an investigation and autopsy to make sure there was no medical malpractice to blame. Therefore, her IV would still be in and tubes down her throat. I guess he wanted me to be aware of those things, so I was not too shocked when I saw her. We got to the end of the hallway and came to a room that was dark inside. There was an orderly standing outside the door. I didn't realize why he was there until later. The nurse walked up to the orderly and whispered something that I couldn't hear. He opened the door and stepped back to allow us access to the room.

There were no lights on in the room. The only illumination was coming from the two windows opposite the door we had just came in. I could see Jennifer was lying there in the hospital bed. I guess one could think maybe she was just sleeping, but with the IV's and tubes coming out of her, it made it hard to forget the reason why we were there.

When I was a teenager living in Iowa, there was a particular family that I was a consistent baby-sitter for. They had three young kids with the eldest being eleven years old. Those children could be a handful at times, especially the eldest Jimmy, because we were so close in age. He would often give me a hard time when I was taking care of them. However, since I was able to manage Jimmy, as well as his brothers and sisters, his parents hired me on a pretty regular basis. Unfortunately, one evening, the parents decided to leave Jimmy in charge and therefore, did not call me to baby-sit. I found out the next morning that Jimmy had accidentally hung himself. His younger sister, who found him, had to cut him down, but not before Jimmy had passed away. My mother informed me that when the parents arrived home to the news of Jimmy's death, the father punched the wall so hard that he put a hole in it. Then, when the coroner was trying to remove the body from the house, the father threw a chair and wouldn't let them remove Jimmy's body.

It was with that knowledge that I look back and am surprised by my own reaction at seeing my daughter lying there in that room. I would have thought, like Jimmy's parents, I might have screamed, cried hysterically, grabbed hold of her and refused to let her go or something dramatic like that, but I did none of those things. We stepped inside the room, and my ex went to stand on the right side of her, and I was on her left. I remember that I was crying softly and that I just kept saying, "Why?" over and over again. I remember stroking her hair and thinking how small and frail she looked lying there in that bed. She looked like a little girl and not a woman of twenty-two. My baby girl! How was this happening? I told her how very much I loved her and how I was going to miss her every single day she was gone. My ex just stood there not saying or doing anything. I think he was just too shocked to even know what to say or do.

After several minutes, the nurse came back in and asked if we are ready to go. Are you ever ready to leave when saying your final farewell to your child? I think not! Yet there I was, kissing my baby girl's forehead one last time and slowly heading toward the door.

As I reached the end of the bed, I saw Jennifer's socked foot was sticking out from under the blanket. Without even a thought, I caressed her foot as I passed it by. A mother's final loving touch of her daughter, forever! Such a simple gesture and yet one that is locked in my brain for all of eternity.

While the nurse led the way, we shuffled back to the "family room." I was surprised to see Kathy still had not shown up. I wondered where she was. An uncomfortable mood settled over the room, and the conversation lagged between all of us. At that point my estranged husband's girlfriend encouraged my ex that he should head for home. There was nothing more we could do at the hospital. She was right, of course, but I think for both of us, it felt like we were abandoning our child there. That was a moment that no parent should ever have to face.

We quickly discussed the funeral arrangements, and then we all exited the room. My ex, his girlfriend, and his sister all headed in one direction, while I was left standing there wondering where I should go next. The nurse who had been helping us came over and asked if she could be of any assistance. I explained that I was waiting for my friend who had brought me to the hospital. The nurse, being the kind person that she was, led me over to a sitting area near the emergency room doors. She sat down with me and tried to make small talk. However, I was really in no mood for talking to anyone at that point. After a few minutes of awkward silence, she rose and said she needed to get back to work. I thanked her for her kindness. She left me sitting there lost in my own thoughts.

Finally, Kathy appeared. She apologized profusely for having left me alone for so long, but she had a terrible time finding a parking spot. She finally had to park on the other side of the hospital, and then she had gotten lost trying to find me. I explained to her that I was ready to go and that I had already seen Jennifer. She wrapped her arms around me and gave me a hug for moral support. She apologized once again for not being there for me, but I let her know it was okay.

We walked back through the hospital in the direction from which Kathy had just come. That route took us back past the family room I had just been in, as well as the room that Jennifer laid in. Once again, I noticed that same orderly standing outside the door. It was at that moment that it slowly dawned on me why he was there. *So, no one would steal her body.* I had an overwhelming impulse to rush past him and back into that room, to see my daughter once again. I fought the hysteria that crept over me and just kept slowly following Kathy down the hall. My own personal turmoil was running rampant within me.

We weaved and crisscrossed many hallways to make our way toward the back of the hospital. As we reached the exit doorway, I happened to see something shiny lying on the ground just on the other side of the sliding doors. As Kathy and I stepped through them, I bent down to see what it was. It was a dime. "Huh, that's strange," I thought to myself as I absent mindedly picked it up and placed it into my pocket. However, my mind was elsewhere, so I didn't give it any further thought.

Once we were outside, Kathy informed me that her car was parked up a large hill in a parking garage. I must have looked like hell at that point, because she pointed to a nearby bench and suggested that I have a seat while she went to go get the vehicle. I was in no mood to argue with her, so I shrugged okay and slowly trudged over to sit down. I was still in a daze from all that had happened to me that day. As I went to collapse onto the bench, something peculiar caught my eye, lying on the ground between my feet. I bent over and picked it up. It was another dime. How strange that was, two dimes in such a short amount of time. "Why?" I pondered, as I slowly played with the coin I had just picked up. Like a curtain at a play that begins to rise, the foggy veil was lifted from around my brain momentarily and it slowly began to dawn on me. All those dimes I had found in the past month, they were God's way of preparing me for that very moment. He knew that I would need something, anything, to cling to for getting me through this nightmare. At that very moment, through God's grace, I came to realize that life _does_ continue after a death for all of us, both the living and the deceased. That those who passed away can sometimes leave us little reminders that they are still around and watching over us. My sign from Jennifer would be dimes. As this knowledge slowly crept into my brain, it was the one comfort that would help me to move on, as the days and weeks went by. Of course, God in his infinite wisdom knew that I would need something, anything to hold onto, to be able to survive losing my child.

CHAPTER
4

THE CHRISTMAS MIRACLE

Two weeks after Jennifer's death, Joseph graduated from high school. That was such a bittersweet day for all of us. On one hand, we were thrilled for Joe and all that he had accomplished, but on the other, our hearts were still aching so badly from missing Jen. It was difficult to not allow the pain to show through. Plus, we did not want to dampen what should have been a happy occasion for my son. One of Joseph's Navy recruiters came to lend moral support to all of us, which we truly appreciated. While we were walking into the auditorium where Joe's graduation was to be held, I found a dime lying in the street. Finding that dime helped my family and me to know that Jennifer was there watching over her little brother on his very special day. It was a small symbol of hope, but it offered a great comfort to everyone. Something we all desperately needed to help us make it through that day.

I don't really remember much about those first few months after Jennifer's death and Joseph's graduation. Looking back, it all blurs into one miserable day after another. There are bits and pieces that stick out but not a complete picture. Each day was a huge emotional and mental struggle to make it through.

Shortly after Joe's graduation, my parents had to return to Texas which left Joseph and me to deal with our own personal grief. Joseph had gotten a part time job at that time. So, between his working and hanging out with his friends, I didn't get to see him much. I was often alone at night which didn't help matters. Tim came to visit as often as he could from Pennsylvania. However, he still had to work, so he wasn't able to stay as long as either one of us would have liked. It was a very sad and lonely time for me. I often cried myself to sleep at night. The pain in my heart was almost more than I could bear. How I had the strength to go on, I do not truly know, but go on I did. Each painful day slipped into the next. The only thing that truly kept me moving along at all was finding the dimes and clinging to them as a constant reminder that my beloved Jennifer was still with me, at least in spirit. If I hadn't had that, and my faith, to help me through, I am not sure I would have survived that awful period of my life. Losing a child, I believe to be one of the most devastating things that could ever happen to a person.

As the months slowly progressed one into the next, I found myself facing the approaching holiday season. I was not looking forward to it at all. I was in no mood to celebrate anything, least of all Christmas. All those family get-togethers, gift giving and joyous celebrations, just one big constant reminder of everything I had lost. Plus, I was finding that some people were acting strange toward me because my daughter had passed away. I don't know if it was because they were afraid they would do or say something that might upset me. But then, some even had the gall to insinuate that maybe it shouldn't have affected me as much as it did since my daughter and I were estranged from one another. But I think that almost made things worse, since we never had a chance to reconcile our differences. Now, there would be no hope for reconciliation, which hurt just about as much as losing her did. Whatever the reason was, people were pulling away from me when I needed them the most. Then to add insult to my already aching heart, I had one very bad experience at the school where I worked.

It was the second week of December when I was called into my principal's office. She informed me that some of my fellow colleagues had been complaining to her that my sadness was bringing the school down. She told me that I needed to cheer up and in a hurry. She felt I had grieved long enough, and now it was time to move on. How dare she? How did she know that enough time had passed for my grieving? Each person's grieving process is different. It was not even a year since Jennifer's death. That from the same group of people who told me they would be there for me if I needed anything, anything at all! But now my sadness was ruining their holiday spirit. How was I supposed to be happy when I had just lost my daughter only six months earlier? I have to admit that I truly do not understand people sometimes.

Around the middle of the third week of December, my son Joseph received an early Christmas present from a member of his father's family. It was a silver ornament, shaped like a bell, with an angel sitting on top of it. My estranged husband and his family loved celebrating Christmas. They adored anything that had to do with the holiday season, including Christmas movies. One of their favorites was the movie entitled "It's a Wonderful Life" with Jimmy Stewart. In that movie there was a scene where George Bailey's (Jimmy Stewart) guardian angel, Clarence, explained that every time a bell rang, an angel would get its wings. Therefore, the premise of the angel bell gift was that if Joseph were to ring the bell, it might help Jennifer receive her wings.

For some unknown reason, that symbol and the explanation behind it truly touched me. I found myself liking the idea so much that I approached Tim with the proposal of purchasing a quantity of these ornaments. I had decided that I wanted to give them away as gifts to all our family and friends as a way to remember Jennifer. Tim was in agreement that giving those as a gift would be a nice idea.

Now, one must understand that I hate crowds. So much so, that I do my holiday shopping all year round, just so I don't have to go into the stores at Christmas time. But now I was faced with having to head into a busy mall at the worst possible time of the year. However, I *really* wanted to get those ornaments.

So, the Sunday before Christmas, Tim and I headed off to the local mall. Just trying to find a parking spot was a nightmare. After we drove around looking for a place to park, we finally found an available space a good distance away from the mall entrance. I was just thankful we could find a spot to park at all. We tried to not get run over in the parking lot, as we slowly made our way into the shopping establishment. It was worse than I had anticipated. There were people everywhere! Mothers, fathers, crying babies, running toddlers and teenagers. More than I could even begin to count. All I wanted to do was get the ornaments and get the heck out of there.

Tim and I slowly weaved our way through the throngs of holiday shoppers. Christmas music was blaring from every store and throughout the entire mall. My head was pounding, and it was difficult for me to breathe being in such a crowded space. If it wasn't for those darn ornaments, I wouldn't be there at all.

We finally located the store that carried the ornament and proceeded up to the third floor by use of the escalator. After a bit of searching, Tim and I were able to locate the Christmas section in that very large department store. Luckily for us, we found the ornaments that we were searching for. Thankfully, there were more than enough for what we wanted. Tim and I gathered up as many ornaments as we could carry. Then, with me leading the way, we carefully headed towards a check-out register. We crisscrossed our way through the holiday displays and tables full of Christmas decorations. As I began to leave the carpeted

Christmas section for the tiled aisle way, I heard and felt my foot kick something. I looked down to observe an ornament rolling out onto the tiled floor. Fearing that someone might step on it and break it, I bent down to pick it up and place it somewhere safe. As I awkwardly juggled my load of ornaments, I noticed that there was something written on the ornament I had just picked up. I turned it, so I could see what it said. In big black letters, the name, "Jennifer" stared back at me! I almost dropped everything in my arms as I was so stunned by what it was I was seeing. Meanwhile, Tim having heard the ornament hit the tile floor, was just about to give me a hard time for wrecking the joint when he saw my expression. The shock of what I had just seen was quite apparent on my face. He rushed over to me, as he couldn't imagine what could possibly be wrong. With tears streaming down my face, I slowly turned the ornament around so that Tim could read what it said. With a look of dismay, he said to me, "Well, I guess we are buying that one too?" Like he even had to ask. What were the odds? Tim and I looked to see if we could find any more of that same type of ornament in the immediate vicinity, but with no luck. How very strange.

After we searched for any more of the "Jennifer" ornaments, Tim and I headed to the check-out counter to pay for all our merchandise. There was of course, a long line at the register. As we proceeded to get in the back of the line, Tim informed me that he was going to go see if he could find out where the "Jennifer" ornament might have come from.

While he was off looking, the line slowly inched its way forward toward the register. After much time had passed, it finally became my turn to see the cashier and to pay for my items. As I approached the check-out I saw something shiny lying on the floor in front of the counter. I couldn't believe my eyes; it was a dime. Like the ornament hadn't been clear enough, Jen had to be sure I knew she was there. I just shook my head in shear amazement as I bent down to claim that dime. Why hadn't any of the other shoppers seen the coin and picked it up? In my mind it meant only one thing… that the dime was meant solely for me. It took everything I had not to burst into tears once again while standing there as my purchases where rung up and I waited to pay.

At that point, Tim finally returned to the check-out counter. I showed him the dime I had just found and the spot on the floor where I had retrieved it from. He just shook his head in disbelief. He said to me, "I finally found the stand where the "Jennifer" ornament should have come from. It was clear across the store from where we were. Not to mention, the spot for "Jennifer" was completely empty. I truly believe that Jennifer understood why we were purchasing those special angel ornaments and that she was happy that people would have something to remember her by.

I still have that dime that I retrieved from the floor that day at the mall. It is glued to the bottom of the "Jennifer" ornament that we also found that day. I keep it out, displayed all year, as a gentle reminder that miracles do happen in very strange ways. Least of all, when we do not expect them.

CHAPTER 5

BELIEVE IN ANGELS

The angel ornament was a huge hit with our friends and family. Everybody was extremely touched to have received such a memorable gift. They thought it was a wonderful idea and a great way to remember Jennifer. Each year when they go to decorate their Christmas tree and pull out that special angel bell, each one of them will think of Jen. That helped ease my heartache just a little bit, knowing my sweet baby girl would never be forgotten.

I have always believed in angels, even before Jennifer's death. Since I was raised in a Catholic household, there were lots of religious artifacts throughout my childhood homes. Those items included a picture of an adolescent boy and girl crossing a bridge, with an angel flying over them as their protector. That image always touched me in a very special way. As a child growing up, the idea of knowing we are protected by God's guardian angels was very comforting to me. Now with my sweet daughter's passing, my belief that she was in heaven watching down over us as a possible angel truly helped me get through some of the tougher days. I am grateful that Tim believes the same way I do.

Tim's mother is also a big believer in angels. She has some very beautiful pictures and a statue collection of all types of angels in various shapes and sizes. So, it was no real surprise when she presented Tim and me with a wooden plaque with a saying about angels. It was about three feet long and engraved with the words "We Believe in Angels." She told us that as soon as she saw it, she just knew she would have to get it for Tim and me. She informed us that she thought it would look really nice in our new house that Tim and I were working to fix up, so we could move into it. We happened to agree with her. However, we weren't ready to move in just then, so we wrapped up the plaque and put it away for safe keeping until we were able to put it on display in our new home.

Once Tim and I became engaged, we decided that I would complete my ten years with the school district on Long Island. After that, if I still had not found a job in Pennsylvania, I would move there anyway. That would allow me to start my new life with Tim, as well as, try to get a divorce through another state. I would have to be a permanent resident of the state with a valid Pennsylvania license for six months before I would be able to pursue anything on the divorce front. That was fine with me as nothing was progressing in New York anyway. Plus, all I really wanted at that point was to move to Pennsylvania and be with Tim.

So, I finished up my ten years of working on Long Island, said good-bye to some loyal friends and headed to Pennsylvania to my new life with my fiancé, Tim. Once I was settled in Pennsylvania, the hunt for work continued. I had been looking for a while from New York, but I hadn't had any luck. I did have a few interviews but unfortunately nothing that turned into a job offer. Now that I was actually living in Pennsylvania I was hoping that would enable me to find some work here faster. Within a month, I was fortunate to get a secretarial job in a small elementary school just twenty minutes away from our future new home. How very blessed was I?

Now that I had moved and found a new job, we were able to focus all our energy on getting the improvements done on our future new domain. Every weekend that we had free, meant time spent cleaning; painting; carpentry work; home repair and so on. We worked hard and were exhausted at the end of each day, but we felt accomplished in knowing that we would reach our goal of being able to move in shortly. Each time we headed over to the house to work, we brought with us at least one car load of boxes, furniture and whatever else we felt we could bring over. That enabled us to unpack the boxes and put things away immediately where we wanted them to go. The closer we got to moving in, the more items we were bringing over from the old house that my honey and I were staying in.

One particular weekend, Tim and I had made several trips back and forth between the two houses. On one of the final trips of the weekend, I came across the wooden plaque from Tim's mother. I determined it was time to bring that gift over and hang it up. We had decided earlier that the perfect spot for that item was a wooden archway that led from our living room into our dining room. Therefore, anyone who entered our new home to visit us would see that decoration hanging there and discern that Tim and I believed in angels. So, with the next car load of household items, I made sure that wooden plaque was taken over to the new residence.

Once Tim and I arrived at the house, we parked in the same spot we had been parking in all day. I grabbed the "Angel" plaque off the top of some of the boxes we had brought in the back of the car. As I stepped out of the vehicle, I lost my grip on the gift, and it began to fall towards the pavement. "Oh, no," I thought to myself. "Not the Angel plaque!" With quick reflexes, I was able to catch it before it hit the ground. However, as I recovered from that near accident, I was flabbergasted to see that at the very spot that decoration would have hit the pavement laid *a dime*. Really? What were the odds? Needless to say, I scooped up that dime and ran into the house to show it to Tim. We both marveled at the fact that we never noticed it, all those times we parked in the same exact location. I guess Jennifer was trying to let us know that she was around and maybe approved of the new house? One could only speculate. However, the sight of that dime was once again a real solace for me, as well as for Tim. Not to mention the fact that we both believed we had our own personal guardian angel up in heaven watching over us.

If you come to visit Tim and me today, you will find that "Angel" plaque hanging over the archway, just like we wanted it to. It is placed between our living room and dining room for all to see when they enter our home. Glued in the center of the plaque between the words "believe" and "in" is that dime I found that day. The dime, a symbol of what I truly consider being a sign from my daughter, Jennifer. A constant reminder to both Tim and me that, yes, we truly do believe in Angels!

CHAPTER 6

FORGIVENESS IS GIVEN

In the beginning of this book I made mention of the trials I went through trying to dissolve my marriage in New York state. Since that time, eight years had gone by with no results. At that point, I had pretty much given up any hope that I was ever going to get legally separated from my former husband. Fortunately for me, that issue did not seem to bother Tim. He informed me that when it was meant to be, the divorce would happen, and he was ok with waiting. My sweetheart explained that we could still be together as he knew I loved him and only him. That wonderful support and reassurance from Tim helped to relieve some of the pressure for me but it was so difficult when dealing with everyday issues. I never realized the simple things we take for granted, like visiting a doctor's office for the very first time and filling out medical forms. Questions like: "Are you married, widowed, divorced," became complicated. Emergency contact information: "What is your relationship to said person?" It is so much easier when you are legally married and can simply say, "That is my husband," and leave it at that.

Since we were unable to get married legally but wanted to really commit to one another, we decided to have a simple Native American ceremony that would bind our love for each other and our commitment as a couple. We worked with someone at the rafting company whose husband was from the Lenape Nation. Therefore, she was friends with a member of the tribe who performed wedding ceremonies. What was even better, was he was licensed through the state of Pennsylvania to perform judicial weddings, so once I did finally get my divorce he would be able to sign the papers for us to be lawfully married.

October 7, 2012, I married my best friend, the man of my dreams and my perfect soul mate. We had decided to just make it a simple service and incorporated some of the Lenape Nation's traditions into our ceremony. We exchanged our vows to one another standing on the banks of the Delaware River. It was a drizzly and overcast day but neither one of us cared. All that mattered was our pledge to one another under the eyes of our Creator. It was one of the happiest days of my life. A memory that I will carry with me always.

Since I had moved to Pennsylvania, professed my commitment of love to Tim and found employment, all I still had left to do was to get my driver's license so that the countdown to becoming a Pennsylvania resident could begin. Hopefully, once my six months were up, all I needed to do was find a lawyer and try to finally get that elusive divorce. While we were waiting for the time to pass, both Tim and I were asking people we knew if they could recommend a good divorce attorney. One name seemed to keep popping up. So, Tim and I made a decision to give that lawyer a try and hope for the best.

I was extremely nervous about starting the divorce process all over again. The first time in New York had taken such a toll on me both mentally, as well as physically. Plus, it had torn my immediate family apart. My two daughters where so distraught over their father and me separating that they refused to speak to me once I had moved out of the house. Then Jennifer passed away before she and I had a chance to reconcile. "What would this attempt bring," I wondered. Nevertheless, as scared and nervous as I was, I knew I had to go through with it if I wanted to move on with my new life with Tim. I could only hope and pray that God would be with me, guiding me each step of the way. I was also extremely thankful that I had Tim for moral support.

As time passed and my six months of residency came to fruition I made the call to the recommended attorney's office. I was pleased to learn that particular lawyer was accepting new clients and would be happy to meet with Tim and me. Her secretary issued a date and time for us to assemble at the office. My hope was we would learn how that attorney might be able to help me. It was decided that Tim and I would rendezvous at the attorney's building the day of the appointment, as we would be coming from our respective jobs that were in opposite directions from one another.

The day of the meeting arrived, and I was a stressed-out mess. My mind raced with so many questions. "What would the lawyer say?" "Could she even represent me?" "How much would it cost?" "Could Tim and I even afford it?" "Would my daughters ever forgive me?" "Would I ever be able to move on with my life?" All those thoughts and so many more were running rampant through my head when I finally met up with Tim in front of the attorney's office. Tim must have sensed my stress because as soon as he saw me, he gave me a huge bear hug and told me everything would be all right. Oh, how I wished that would be true.

The attorney's business was located in a row home in one of the many patch towns located in that part of the state. Row homes were very prevalent due to the fact that they were owned by the area's coal mining companies. Those businesses used that type of housing for employed coal miners and their families. The one in particular that housed the lawyer's office had been refurbished. It had beautiful stained-glass windows and a wooden overlaid turret. That house definitely had been a masterpiece in its era.

Tim and I proceeded up the front steps, through the hand carved front door and into the plush office beyond. We were met by the lawyer's administrative assistant. She was an elderly woman with a warm smile and what seemed like a gentle disposition. Her demeanor helped to put me a little more at ease. She informed us that the attorney would be with us shortly and to have a seat. The secretary pointed to a row of folding chairs that were lined up against one wall of the office. Tim and I turned away from the secretary's desk and walked over to sit down. As I began to sit, something circular under my chair caught my eye. I bent over to ascertain what it could be. I was astonished to see it was a dime.

At that moment, all the stress, fears, and angst that I had been feeling washed away, leaving me with a wonderful sense of inner peace. Peace in knowing, my heavenly daughter had forgiven me and wanted to see me move on with my life as well. Jennifer had the thoughtfulness to let me know she was around and watching out over me. She must have seen how happy Tim makes me and how good we are together. By my finding that dime, it was her way of letting me know she was okay with why I was there and what it was I was trying to get done.

As I sat up, Tim saw the tears in my eyes and expressed his concern until I slowly opened up my hand and revealed to him what I had just found. He smiled, gave me another comforting hug and said, "See, I told you everything was going to be ok." With my new found inner peace and an angel named Jennifer by my side, I knew he was correct.

It turned out the lawyer was a wonderful woman, who was extremely sympathetic and helpful. She couldn't believe the ordeal that I had gone through with trying to get my divorce in New York. The attorney assured me she would be able to help dissolve my marriage and she was true to her word.

A few months later the divorce was final. I couldn't believe it! It seemed like it had to be a dream, but deep down I felt that there was a heavenly angel that helped to get it resolved. It had taken almost nine years to finally get to that point but now, Tim and I were free to make our marriage official. Finally, this was the end to one chapter of my life and the start of a new one. A new one as Mrs. Barbara Acker!

JENNIFER'S DIMES

CHAPTER 7

MUSIC OF AN ANGEL

As I stated previously, I liked to walk during my lunch hour when the weather was nice. So, it was no coincidence that on a beautiful spring day in 2013 I found myself taking a walk around the neighborhood near my new school in Pennsylvania. The birds were singing, and the warmth of the sun felt terrific on my face. I was glad to be able to get out and walk after a long winter of snow and ice. Cabin fever had set in pretty well for everyone, including myself. So now that spring had finally arrived, I wanted to get out and enjoy every moment that I could.

As I was walking, my mind wandered to thoughts of my sweet Jennifer. In a couple of months, it would be the second anniversary of her passing. It was still so difficult for me to believe that she was gone, let alone for two whole years. I was contemplating if I wanted to travel with Tim to New York on that day. On one hand, I wanted to visit and remember my baby girl, but on the other hand, I was afraid of all the emotions that visiting her grave would invoke in me. I could have just called a local florist and have them send flowers over to the cemetery to be placed on her grave site. But then, there was her memorial tree and engraved plaque that we had set up at her high school, which I really wanted to see. However, I was just not sure I could handle seeing either one of those places. No one should have to make decisions like those. It was a mother's worst nightmare come true.

It was with those thoughts rattling around in my brain that I was aimlessly walking along the back streets behind my school. Suddenly, something glistening in the sun's rays on the side of the road caught my eye. I walked over to where it laid and bent down to see what it was. I was pleasantly surprised to see it was a dime. "Really," I had thought to myself, as I leaned over to pick it up. I couldn't help but just shake my head in sheer amazement. I guess that Jennifer was aware that I was thinking about her. She sure could get my attention and remind me that she was around when I needed it most. I can't begin to explain how finding those dimes at the most opportune times could help me get through some of those rough patches.

I held that dime in my hand as I finished my walk. All the while I talked to my daughter in my head. I just wanted her to know how very much I loved and missed her. Plus, now that I had found that dime it gave me the courage I needed to make the decision to go to New York after all and to place those anniversary flowers on her grave in person. I truly felt that was what Jennifer would like for me to do, so I would honor her wish.

Now, I have to say that as much as I believe those dimes are signs from Jennifer, there are times when the practical side of me comes out. I have to truly wonder if the dimes are signs or just coincidences. Are they just something for a desperate mother missing her child to grasp a hold of? How does one truly know? I guess that is where "Faith" comes into play. Having "faith" enough to believe in a life after this one. But there again, it never seems to fail that when I begin to question the dimes and their purpose, I receive another sign. A message from above just to let me know that "YES" the dimes are from my beautiful daughter.

That was true that day as well. Once I had finished my walk and talk with Jennifer (in my head,) I went back into the school building. On the counter in front of my desk was sitting the day's mail that had arrived while I was out walking. As I sorted the mail into the teacher's mailboxes, I came across a monthly magazine that we had been receiving for some unknown reason. The magazine, entitled "Leatherheads" was a periodical designed around the "US Marine Corp." In it were articles about Marines, their battle stories, different guns and artillery used by that particular armed forces. That was not the type of magazine an elementary school should have been receiving. When that same magazine had arrived the previous month, I had spoken to our assistant principal about it. He liked to hunt and was someone I considered a burly kind of man, so I thought maybe that magazine was coming for him. However, when I questioned him about it, he informed me that he knew nothing about the publication or why it was coming to our school. I asked if he would be interested in seeing it, but he told me, "No." So, with that, I inquired what he wanted me to do with it, and he instructed me to do whatever I wanted to with it. I tried to find someone on our staff who be interested in looking at that type of magazine but with no luck. So, when I saw that month's issue mixed in with the rest of the mail, I tossed it onto the counter with the intention of throwing it away once I was done sorting the mail.

Once I was done distributing the day's mail, I turned to retrieve the "Leatherneck" periodical to throw it away. To my shock and dismay, I found it had fallen open to a page that advertised a music box from the Bradford Exchange. That was strange enough in itself, but what really caught my eye, was the main title of the ad which read "My Daughter, I Love You, Today, Tomorrow, and Always!" "What in the world was an ad like that doing in a US Marine Corps magazine?" I had wondered. I had to take a closer look. Suddenly, my heart skipped a beat! There on the top of the music box was a heart that could be engraved with a person's name. The name the ad had chosen to use? "Jennifer!" What were the chances that they would pick that particular name? I could only assume once again, that this was my Jennifer's way of letting me know that "Yes," the dimes are signs from her, and I am to believe in them.

Needless to say, I have kept that issue of the "Leatherneck" magazine with that Bradford Exchange ad in it. I also ordered that special music box with "Jennifer's" name on it to hold all the dimes that I have been finding and collecting.

As a side note, since that day of finding that particular ad, I have checked every month when that magazine arrives, and there has never been that same advertisement in that magazine ever again. Go figure.

CHAPTER
8

SHE ALWAYS KNOWS

It never ceases to amaze me how Jennifer constantly seems to know when I am thinking of, missing or reminiscing about her. She repeatedly lets me experience that she is aware of my thoughts through her signature dimes. It is so wonderful how a simple dime can give me such great comfort and joy. All of it just amazes me.

One example of that support was when the second anniversary of Jen's passing was upon us. I had made the decision that Tim and I would make the three-hour journey to Long Island, New York. We were headed to place flowers on her grave, as well as visit the memorial we had erected at the high school from which Jennifer had graduated.

Jen *adored* where she went to high school. She enjoyed attending school so much that she went to college to become a math professor. Her dream was to someday be able to teach students at her former high school. She was actually student teaching at that very institution when she passed away. I found some peace in knowing that Jennifer had been able to realize her dream before her life was tragically cut short.

Because Jennifer loved that school so much, Tim, my son Joe, and I, along with donations I had received at the time of Jen's death, planted a blossoming cherry tree in her honor at the front of the high school building. We had a memorial stone created with an etching of Jennifer's likeness, along with the following quote: "No farewell words were spoken… No time to say goodbye…You were gone before we knew it… And only God knows why." That stone was placed in front of the tree we had planted along with two flowering azalea bushes positioned on either side of the memorial. The school administration had been kind enough to give us a wonderful location right in front of the main building, next to the sidewalk that people used to enter the school. Such prominence I could never have imagined. Now my beautiful and amazing daughter would always be remembered.

The school was positioned on a very busy road, and parking could be treacherous at times. As it happened, my son had opened up a savings account at a bank that was located directly across the street from the high school. Since Joe was away in the Navy, he had some banking issues he needed us to take care of for him. Tim and I decided that it would be easier for us to park in the bank's parking lot, take care of Joe's issues, and then walk across the street to the high school to visit the memorial.

After we finished our business at the bank, it was time to walk over to the high school. The road we had to cross was extremely busy that day, as usual. We decided to walk down to the light, so we could access the cross walk. However, after a few seconds of walking, we noticed there was a break in the traffic. Tim and I decided to make a mad dash for it and cross from where we were. Yes, it would be jay walking, but sometimes you just have to go for it. As we scurried across the four lanes of traffic, something lying in the road in front of me glistened at me in the sunlight. I bent to see what it could be. I was floored when I saw it was a dime. I quickly picked it up. All the while, Tim was yelling at me to hurry up as the traffic had started to descend upon us. We reached the other side of the street and Tim wanted to know what was so important that I had to stop in the middle of the road. I opened up my hand and showed him the dime. He just shook his head in amazement.

What were the chances that we would cross that piece of road at that exact spot to find that dime? It is those types of coincidences that cause me to truly believe the dimes are evidence from my daughter that she is still around and watching over us.

Another perfect example of Jen just knowing I needed that extra reassurance from her came just this past summer. Tim and I were working a very busy weekend at the rafting company. As a wonderful coincidence, there was a Boy Scout and a Girl Scout troop from my old home town on Long Island that where there for the weekend to camp and raft. One of the leaders from the Girl Scout troop happened to be a good friend of mine. She and I had been very involved in scouting together when I used to live on Long Island. She also personally knew my daughters. I was very excited to have this opportunity to see my old friend.

Of course, with both of those troops being from my old home town there was a lot of conversations with people about who knew who and who went to school with whom. By the end of Saturday night, all the talking about Jennifer was really starting to take its toll on me. It was nice to see old friends and reminisce but at the same time it could be very difficult for me, emotionally. I found the ache in my heart, which I was usually able to contain, getting the best of me.

Saturday evening, I met my old Girl Scout buddy and her scouts at one of our covered pavilions that wasn't used very often. There was a special animal program being held there for the scouts. I wanted to visit with my friend for a little while longer before I had to leave for the night. Of course, as we were talking the conversation turned to Jennifer once more and how very much I missed her. All of the emotions that had been building the entire day hit me like an avalanche and I broke down crying. My friend placed her arms around my shoulders, gave me a hug and some much-needed support. We sat like that for a few minutes as I tried to collect myself. As I slowly raised my head to dry my tears, I noticed something round lying amongst the rocks under the picnic table across from us. "No, it couldn't be," I had thought to myself. I moved over to get a closer look. I just couldn't believe it. There lying amidst the dirt, pebbles and leaves was a dime. A beaten up and weathered worn dime, but still a dime all the same. Once again, Jennifer surprised me by showing me that she was aware of my pain. Finding that dime was her way of trying to give me some peace of mind with letting me know that she was still around. Why else would I find a dime in a place like that and at that exact moment when I needed it most.

The last really good example that Jennifer let me know she was watching out over me happened at my 50th birthday party. Since my birthday falls on the day after Christmas, most of my life I have been short- changed when it comes to celebrating. Some of the reasons were: too many holiday affairs to attend; people forget because they are just too busy with worrying about Christmas; and family or friends aren't around to be able to help me celebrate at that particular time of the year. Whatever the reason, my birthday has become an issue for me. It is a day I do not look forward to each year. I say to myself that I will not let it bother me, and every year it still does. I am not sure I will ever get over it, but I am trying. It does help that I am now married to Tim, who desperately tries to make it a very special day for me. Because of Tim's caring and planning, a 50th birthday party came to fruition for me a couple years ago.

It happened that my son, Joseph, was granted leave from the Navy to come home over the that Christmas break. Since his father and I were now divorced and living in two different states, Joe planned to split his time between New York and Pennsylvania. I wanted him to have time with his father, but I also wanted to see him as much as I could. Tim and I decided that we would take him to New York several times, since he did not have a vehicle of his own. One of those visits fell on my birthday.

Ever since I lived on Long Island, there was a wonderful establishment that I liked to go to called "Dave & Buster's." It was a place where you could enjoy good food, play hundreds of awesome arcade games, and watch your favorite sports teams on giant televisions. I had told both Tim and Joe that I would like to have a party there sometime, so that was exactly what they planned for me. Unfortunately, once again because of the time of the year, they were unable to get enough people to attend to be able to rent a private room. However, my good friends Kathy, Victor, Mara and Fred were able to be present, along with Tim and Joe. When I arrived at the venue I was pleasantly surprised to see that there was a small table which had been decked out with birthday balloons and streamers. They even had thought to get me a very yummy birthday cake. After we ate our meal, I opened some gifts, and then they sang "Happy Birthday" to me. We ate the delicious cake with buttercream frosting and then we headed into the arcade to play some games. It was an awesome afternoon spent playing and laughing with some wonderful friends and family.

Unfortunately, before I knew it, the time had come for us to head out and begin our journey back home to Pennsylvania. As our little party was walking out of the arcade area toward the exit of the building, I beheld a dime lying on the carpeted floor. Several of my friends had actually walked over it, not even noticing that it was there. However, I sure couldn't miss it especially since I knew that it was meant for me. Everyone was amazed as I showed them what I had just picked up off of the floor. By that time, they all knew my stories of the dimes and who that wonderful sign was from. My sweet daughter just wanted me to know that she was at my party too and that she was wishing me a "Happy Birthday." I thought to myself, "Thanks Jennifer for making my 50th birthday the best one ever!" I couldn't have asked for a better birthday present.

CHAPTER 9

PASSING ON THE STORY

In the beginning, I didn't tell too many folks about my dime stories. I figured some people either wouldn't believe me or would think that I was totally crazy. Why wouldn't they? At times, I have had my own doubts, as well. Of course, Tim knew, as well as my best friends Kathy and Mara. Also, my son Joseph and my immediate family, but other than that, I pretty much kept it to myself. I didn't want to risk being laughed at or worse yet, to be made fun of for believing what I did. It is difficult enough dealing with the loss of a child. I didn't want to give naysayers another reason to make my life more miserable than it already was. Besides, I figured the dimes were meant for me, from Jennifer, and it didn't matter if others knew or believed what I believed.

However, all that changed one day while I was working at the whitewater rafting company. It was early in the season, so once the rafters headed out for the day, the staff was free to catch a bite to eat or just relax a bit before the onslaught of the returning trips. That particular early summer day was especially gorgeous. It had warmed up nicely but not too hot. There was a soft, gentle breeze and the scent of new flowers filled the air. That is my favorite time of the year. It was so beautiful out that I decided to sit on one of the patio steps outside of the company store and soaked up some of the sun's rays. The warmth of the sun felt good on my face and really helped to lift my spirits. A friend and co-worker, Mary Lou, joined me on the steps. Mary Lou and her husband have been working at the rafting company for years. They both have become good friends to Tim and me. Because of that friendship, they were one of the many recipients who received an angel ornament from us, in remembrance of Jennifer.

While we sat there, Mary Lou and I entered into a conversation. Mostly, we talked about work and the wonderful day we were experiencing. However, in the course of the discussion, Mary Lou revealed to me that she had just recently lost her mother over the past winter and was struggling with all the emotions that came from such a loss. I could tell she was extremely upset over her mother's death, the further we delved into the conversation. She asked me if I wouldn't mind staying and converse with her for a little while, as she was in hopes it might help her to find some peace. I am always willing to help someone, especially anyone who is struggling with the loss of a loved one. I have found from my own experience, that sometimes just talking about it *truly does* seem to help relieve a little bit of the pain in one's heart.

Mary Lou informed me how touched she and her husband Tim had been by receiving the gift of the Christmas ornament. She really thought it was such a great idea, and it truly moved her. She expressed her interest in trying to do something similar to remember her mother. We discussed several different options that she thought might work. I was so thankful that I was there at that right moment to offer her a shoulder to cry on and a listening ear. I hoped in some small way that I was helping her.

As we were talking, the conversation changed to miracles and signs we might receive from the other side. Mary Lou expressed to me her wish that she would get some type of indication from her mother that she was still around and watching over her. I was pleasantly surprised to hear her talk like that. I am never sure if someone feels the same way I do in regard to the afterlife. I decided to take a chance and shared with Mary Lou some of my dime stories, including the one about the ornament I almost stepped on at Christmas time.

Mary Lou was amazed by my account of all the dimes I had found in relationship to my daughter. She informed me that unfortunately, she never finds money, so that type of sign wouldn't work for her. I told her to just keep her eyes open and believe. Maybe something would present itself to her as an indication that "Yes" her mother was still around. One just never knows. My personal feeling was that one just needs to truly believe, and then it would come to pass. But obviously in God's time or our passed loved one's time, not our own. Of course, the waiting for one of those heavenly miracles to bless us can be the worst part of all.

Suddenly, a yellow school bus, filled with returning rafters, rumbled into the whitewater adventure center, which interrupted our conversation. Mary Lou and I jumped to our feet to return to our respective posts. Before we went our separate ways, Mary Lou gave me a huge hug and thanked me for being such a wonderful listener. I felt good that I was able to help her in some small way. She seemed a bit more relaxed than before and not as upset as when we had first begun to talk. Plus, I was thankful that she didn't think me crazy for my dime stories, which was a bonus. Maybe there are other people out there who believe the way I do? One could only hope.

I headed back inside the store to the photo department where I was working. With the return of one of the trips, the rest would be following shortly, so I wanted to be as prepared as possible. I was lost in my preparations when the door to the photo lab burst open and in rushed Mary Lou. She was crying uncontrollably. I sprang from the chair I had been sitting in and ran over to her. All the while, I was asking her what was wrong, but she was not answering me. I couldn't imagine what had happened to bring her to such a state when I had left her perfectly fine, minutes before. As I approached Mary Lou she was still crying and shaking, but she slowly opened her hand to reveal a bright, shiny dime! A dime, she found, not more than two minutes after we had finished our conversation about signs. What were the chances? That from a woman who had declared just minutes before that she never finds money!

Needless to say, the spirits made a believer out of Mary Lou that day, and once again I was reminded how God can work in such mysterious ways. Ways that we will never truly understand until that day we join both God and our loved ones in eternal life.

CHAPTER 10

THE MYSTERIOUS WORK DIMES

I stated earlier, that after moving to Pennsylvania, I was able to find a job working at a small elementary school as an administrative assistant. That school had roughly 250 students enrolled and only served kindergarten and first grade. The faculty consisted of all women, except for the principal and assistant principal. Those administrators floated in and out of the building, as they were responsible for a total of three elementary schools within that district. The environment at that institution was one of "family." Everyone helped each other out whenever there was a need to. When something good or bad happened to one member of the faculty, it felt like it happened to all of us. When I arrived at that school, those lovely women welcomed me into their fold with opened arms. They truly had helped to make me feel right at home there, which had been such a wonderful blessing. Maybe it was because of that awesome environment being what it was that I felt Jennifer was happy for me. Since I had started working at that school, I had several episodes with finding dimes in my assigned work space. Always when I would least expect it.

Shortly after I had become employed at the school, I had my first amazing experience of finding a dime there. It was the middle of the day and I had gotten up from my desk to put some papers into the teachers' mail boxes. Lying on the carpeted floor between the front visitor's counter and the wall was a dime. I was so surprised to see it there, as no one had been through that section of the office for quite some time. I couldn't imagine how that small token had found its way there. Besides, I had been up and down from my desk all day, going through that same area, without ever seeing anything. "How very strange," I had thought to myself. As I had leaned over to pick it up, the speech teacher entered the office. She noticed me bent over and asked what I was doing. I showed her the dime that I had just picked up from off the floor. Like me, she was astonished at where I had found it because it just wasn't a spot where you would find money. I explained to her what the symbolism of the dime meant to me. She was very intrigued and thought it was pretty cool that I received indications like that, that my daughter was around. Finding that dime in that location once again cemented for me my theory of who the dimes came from.

The second time I found a dime at work, it really spooked me because of where and how I found it. I had been sitting at my desk all day doing paper work; inputting data on my computer; and answering phone calls when I had to get up to go use the restroom. When I returned to my desk, lying right next to my phone was a bright, shiny, new dime. Now, like I said, I had been answering the phones all day and there was no dime laying there at any point during that time. "Where in the heck did that one come from," I had thought to myself. "How did it get there?" Sometimes students come into the office and deposit things on my desk even when I am not present, but I couldn't imagine that it was from any of them. There would have been no reason for a student to place a dime on my work station. Then I thought maybe the nurse might have found it and put it there because she was aware of the symbolism of what dimes mean to me. However, when I questioned her about it, she informed me that no, it wasn't from her. I even asked some of the other teachers as they came into the office, but the answer was always "No." Still to this day, I have no idea where or how that dime came to be on my desk. However, I have a picture of my sweet, beautiful Jennifer that sits on my work station and I have glued those special dimes to the corners of the frame, as a gentle reminder to me of how much my daughter loves and cares about me.

The last work dime I found came to pass, just as strangely as the previous ones. Our school was participating in a fundraising event for a special organization. Due to donations being sent in for that event, money was coming into the office from the students on a daily basis. As the only school secretary, it was my job to collect that money, keep track of who sent in what, and to be sure that everything matched up correctly. On that particular day as I was opening up envelopes and checking amounts received, I came upon an envelope that said it had a $50 donation in it. However, as I sliced open the payment envelope a dime fell out and landed on my desk, along with a check. I looked again to see what the payment envelope said the donated amount should have been. It read $50, which was what the check was actually made out for. Nowhere did it state there should have been a dime in the envelope as well. And yet there it sat on my desk staring back at me. Just one more example of Jennifer reaching out to me in an unimaginable way. I did not keep that dime like I normally did but sent it along with the rest of the donated money. It had already done its job without me having to keep it.

JENNIFER'S DIMES

CHAPTER 11

A Sense of Humor

Before I met my husband Tim, I had very little knowledge of NASCAR or what makes up that recreational pastime. However, my sweetie being a huge car guy changed all that for me, once we got together. I learned about auto racing; the drivers that make up the sport and all the other little details that go into being a fan. I was educated about the different tracks and where they are located. One of those raceways is right here in the Poconos of Pennsylvania. I also came to know that Tim has one particular driver that he is a super huge fan of, namely Richard Petty. Regrettably, by the time my husband and I got together Mr. Petty had retired from the sport. However, he is still very active today as an owner of a NASCAR franchise and vehicle #43, which still races under his tutelage.

I have come to learn how to identify my sweetheart's favorite car. From the "Petty Blue" as it is known in the industry to the bright red striping on the sides and hood, and finally the iconic #43 in bold, white paint.

If you were to visit my husband's bachelor home, you would see a large quantity of #43 memorabilia. From race posters; car diecasts (in all shapes and sizes); coffee table books about NASCAR and Richard Petty; Pez dispensers; piggy banks and so much more.

Sadly, I learned that for all the years that Tim has been a fan, he has never had the opportunity to meet his favorite driver. He came close once when Tim and his father went to visit Mr. Petty's museum in Tennessee. They were informed by the curator that Richard had just been in the building to meet and greet some of his fans but had left roughly ten minutes prior to their arrival.

The knowledge of Tim not being able to meet his idol, weighed heavy on my heart. So, when I had the chance to sign up to receive emails from Pocono raceway and NASCAR I jumped at the opportunity. Of course, as you can imagine, the influx of information that began to fill up my online mailbox. Propaganda such as: racing posts; NASCAR paraphernalia for sale; contests to enter; and so much more. Because I acquired so many mailings, I would usually scan them quickly and then delete almost all of them from my inbox.

Somewhere around the first or second week of November 2016 I received an advertisement that really peaked my interest. The message of that specific online correspondence was from a travel agency that had put together a first time ever "NASCAR Cruise." The boat line being used for that venture was the Norwegian Pearl. It would travel out of Miami, Florida; sail to Key West; Nassau, Bahamas; and a private island owned by the cruise ship company. But what really caught my eye was the list of celebrity drivers who would be in attendance on that voyage. Richard Petty was one of them.

As much as that information peaked my interest, I must admit that a few weeks went by before I had a chance to revisit that email and give it some serious thought. By then, it was the first week of December and the trip was scheduled for the last week in January. At that time, I figured my chance to get a couple spots on such a fabulous vacation had come and gone. However, I concluded it wouldn't hurt to give the listed number a call to see what the cost would be and if there were any rooms still available. To my shock and pleasant surprise, the cost of the boat excursion was extremely affordable. Not to mention, there where rooms still available. Nevertheless, time was slowly running out and I needed to make a decision. Normally, something of that magnitude would have been discussed by the two of us, together. But I knew Tim too well. He would never want us to spend so much money on something he would have thought to be too extravagant, especially if it was for his sake. With me, he has no problem spending money on, but not so much when it comes to himself. So, I did the next best thing and talked it over with my son, Joe. Together we decided that an opportunity like that one only came around once in a lifetime and so I should take the plunge and go for it!

It just so happened that in a few months, March 2017 to be exact, Tim would have been turning 50. I had planned to throw him a surprise party for his half century mark. However, my husband is not one who likes to have a lot of attention drawn to himself or a big fuss made over him. So, with those thoughts in mind, it made my decision that much easier. I would forgo the surprise party and treat him to a cruise instead.

I was unsure how to present that special gift to my honey. My original idea was to not tell Tim until the day we would have been leaving for the trip. But there were too many decisions that needed to be made which I did not feel comfortable making all on my own. I felt I really needed Tim's input into those arrangements. Like how would we get to Miami from Pennsylvania, drive or fly? Who would take care of the dog while we were away? How long would or should we go for? So, on and so on. I would have to tell him but how?

I finally settled on Christmas afternoon. Once gifts had been opened and we had had time to celebrate that special day, I would suddenly exclaim I had forgotten a gift. As luck would have it, a couple days before Christmas I was out running errands when I saw a cruise ship ornament for sale in a store window. Perfect! I would wrap up that ornament and give it to Tim along with a letter I had put together. The note had a picture of Richard Petty and was written like it came from him, inviting my husband to come meet him in Miami, on the Norwegian Pearl.

It all went as I had planned. To say my sweetheart was speechless would be an understatement. He actually got teary eyed when he read the pretend correspondence from Mr. Petty. I think he was in total shock for a day or two afterwards.

Once Tim knew, we were able to move forward on making the plans and working out all the little details that would go into making that excursion a reality. Before we knew it, it was time to leave for the adventure of a lifetime!

We had made the decision to drive to Miami instead of flying. That would enable us to stop along the way to show each other sites and historical places we both had seen on our own before we got together but wanted to share with one another.

It took us several days to make it down to Florida, especially because of the stops we made. Once we arrived in Miami we spent the night in a hotel, so we would be near the boat dock for boarding on the following day.

The next day, it seemed to take forever to get through the security check-in and boat loading process but finally, we were on the ship! And what a magnificent ocean liner it was. Of course, it had to be pouring rain that day, so we were soaked and just wanted to get to our state room. Despite longing to do that, we couldn't as our accommodations were not ready. So, we meandered around the various decks that made up that mighty vessel. There was an opening ceremony that happened on the top pool deck but with the downpour being what it was, we only stayed for as long as it took for them to announce our cabin was ready to be accessed. The rest of that day and evening was spent exploring the "Pearl." We stood on a covered deck to watch that mighty beast as it slipped away from its moorings and the brilliant lights of Miami. We headed into the blackness of the moonless night. Our adventure had begun.

The next morning found us already docked at a pier inside a Naval base. At the bottom of the gangplank waited shuttle trams which escorted us off the Navy compound and into the heart of Key West. The sun was shining brightly, and a cool breeze blew through the palm trees, making a sweet rustling sound. Tim and I spent the day playing tourist, all to our hearts' content. We explored the many intriguing sights and landmarks that make up that wonderful little town. By late afternoon, we found our way to a local beach where I got to spend several hours looking for and collecting shells and small pieces of coral. While I did that, my hubby relaxed, took pictures, and just watched the rolling waves as they crashed onto the shoreline. As you could probably guess, both of us were in our own perfect heaven. To top off that fantastic day, we were privileged to witness one of the most spectacular and gorgeous sunsets that I think either one of us had ever seen! The icing on the cake, as they would say.

The following day we found out the ship had traveled through the night once again, and we awoke to find ourselves docked at a new pier. Nassau, Bahamas was our venue of choice that day. A normal dock greeted us as we exited the "Pearl," so no shuttle trams were required. Instead we could walk ourselves down the gang way and out into the local community. As we had done the day before, Tim and I just wandered up and down the streets checking out all the different store fronts as something would catch our eye or peak our interest.

Finally, we saw a sign for a local ocean front park which beckoned to us. Isn't that what a vacation is all about? As Tim found a comfortable, shady spot to watch me and the ocean, I began my fruitful search for more sea shells and coral pieces. Once again, I found myself losing my sandals and sinking my toes into some warm beach sand. Shortly, after beginning my hunt something glistening in the water by the shoreline caught my eye. I moved in closer to see what it was. I could tell it was a coin of some type but bigger than dime size, so it couldn't be that. It looked more like a quarter. Which is what I was expecting it to be, as I reached into the water to pluck it from the sandy shoreline. To my awe and utter disbelief, it wasn't a quarter after all. Instead a Bahamian coin stared back at me as I placed it into the palm of my hand for further inspection. The value of that coin I just picked up? Ten cents! I swear I could hear my baby girl laughing!

CHAPTER
12

THE PENN STATE VISIT

Saturday, April 08, 2017 found both Tim and me, along with our dog Maggie, headed out early in the morning to visit my son, Joseph at college. By that point, Joe had done a four-year tour of duty in the Navy and was then into his first year of collegiate studies. He had chosen Penn State as it was close enough to Tim and me but offered all he was looking for in a university without being right in mom's backyard. I of course, was thrilled by the fact that he was now only two hours away from me versus half way around the world, like he had been, while serving this great nation of ours.

Life can be so unpredictable at times. Sometimes, one little decision we make can alter a person's entire life. We may not even realize at the time the decision has been made, that it would have such an impact on our lives but sometimes we do. Take me for instance. If I had not decided to take those kayaking lessons, I would never have gone to work for the whitewater rafting company; would never have met and married my wonderful husband, Tim; nor moved to Pennsylvania. But because I did make that one little decision, everything changed. Now my son was home from the Navy and he was attending a college in PA, instead of New York. That would have never happened if I hadn't taken those kayaking lessons. Crazy, right?

Anyway, getting back to that Saturday in April. It was a gorgeous spring day with the sun playing hide and seek through the white puffy clouds, which gave way to a cool nip in the air. There was the promise of it warming up later in the day as the sun rose higher and warmed the atmosphere. All three of us, including Maggie, enjoyed the beautiful drive to State College. Not to mention the fact that we looked forward to visiting with Joe.

We arrived at Penn State in exactly two hours from the time we left. That was pretty good, considering we had to make a rest area stop for a bathroom break for both Maggie and me. Once we arrived in the parking lot of the student housing unit that my son lived in, I gave Joe a quick call to let him know we had arrived safely. Of course, Joseph being who he is, was not quite ready yet, even though he knew when we were supposed to arrive. Tim, Maggie and I exited the vehicle to stretch our legs and take a small stroll around the parking lot while we waited for my son to come out of his dorm.

After what seemed like an eternity, Joseph finally emerged from his building and walked toward us. After we exchanged hugs, and Joe had a chance to play with Maggie for a moment, we walked back over to where our car was parked. We discussed the fact that it would probably be best if my son drove his vehicle, as it was a much larger automobile and could hold all of us way better than our little red Chevy Sonic.

Now, I have to say that even though my son had done four years in the military, he was still a pack rat and a bit of a slob. This was something that I, as his mother, had hoped would change while he was away in the Navy but alas, that was not to be. Joseph and I proceeded to his car to begin the clean out of debris that was necessary if we were going to use his vehicle. Joe took care of the front seats while I was stuck tackling the middle row. That of course, was where my son threw all his empty food wrappers; meal containers; empty or partially used soda and water bottles. I removed all the empty refuse first, making several trips to a nearby garbage can. Recyclables went next. Finally, I was left with the partially filled water bottles. I didn't want to be wasteful, so I opened the water bottles, walked over to a tree that was located near the sidewalk and began to pour out the left-over water onto the root base of said tree. That particular tree I chose, had a bunch of mulch around its base to help absorb and retain water for that living entity. However, as I poured the water out onto the mulch it slowly washed some of the top layers away. As I watched that happen, I noticed that I seemed to have been uncovering a coin of some type. Because it was dark in appearance and still partially implanted in the mulch, I assumed that it was a penny. At that time, I didn't want to get my hand all dirty by reaching down and picking it up out of the muddy mulch. So, I yelled for Joe to come over and pick up the penny I just uncovered. Joseph begrudgingly did what I asked. However, as he picked it up he turned and looked at me with wide eyes and said, "Mom, that is not a penny. It is a dime!" We both just stared at it for a few seconds and then we walked back over to the car to show Tim.

I guess Jennifer just wanted to let us know that she was there to visit her brother as well. I mean seriously, why did I pick that particular tree to dump the water on, at that very specific spot where I uncovered the dime? I am no math whiz, but I would love to know what the odds would have been for me to find that dime the way that I did. Again, the only real answer that makes any sense to me, was that I was meant to find it because my daughter wanted me to find it.

JENNIFER'S DIMES

CHAPTER 13

The Crayola Experience

If you were to meet Tim and me, you would quickly learn that we love to have fun. Especially simple pleasures like a drive in the country; a walk hand in hand along a beach front; sitting in each other's arms and watching a beautiful sunset; or just going out for a nice inexpensive meal. One of the amazing things about marrying my best friend, is how much we have in common with one another. Because of that, we love to spend as much time together as possible.

We both have a child-like interest in so many diverse things. So, it should come as no surprise that when I learned that the "Crayola" company had a factory tour and crayon fun experience located in nearby Easton, Pennsylvania, it immediately went on my bucket list of something that I wanted to do, especially with my honey. However, with work and just normal everyday life commitments, several years of my living here in PA had gone by and we had not found time to cross this item off my objectives.

One of the many interests that Tim has is anything to do with automobiles. He has loved cars since he was a little boy playing with matchbox toys. He even went so far as to participate in demolition derbies and endure racing with his own vehicles in his twenties. By the time I met my sweetheart, he was no longer involved with those activities. However, when any type of situation arose to watch or explore anything to do with automobiles, we would try to take advantage of it.

So, it happened there was a car show in Bethlehem, PA on a day we were free to check it out. Fortunately, that particular auto show was not too far away from where Tim's mom lives so we were able to kill two birds with one stone by visiting his mother and then heading over to the exhibit.

The presentation of automobiles was almost overwhelming! It was being held on a college campus and was housed in several buildings along with a few outdoor tents. There were new vehicles as well as some very vintage ones. Each one impressive in its own right.

Along with all the cars, there were vendors for all different kinds of items, from auto paraphernalia and accessories, to places to go visit. One of those vendors happened to be the "Crayola Factory" and they were handing out free passes to their experience. Eureka! Now, to just find the time to use them.

It ended up being almost a full year later, when the tickets were about to expire, that we were finally able to make the time to use those free passes.

February 16, 2018 found Tim and myself headed to Easton, Pennsylvania to have our day at the "Crayola Factory." I was so excited. You would have thought I was a little kid and not the 54-year-old woman that I was. Deep down there is still a childlike wonder and awe that I carry with me and pray that I never loose.

Since we already had the free tickets, we were able to enter immediately and begin our day of exploration. With 65,000 square feet of attractions and 25 hands-on activities it was going to be a day of fun, fun, fun! Of course, some of the activities were very much geared to young children but there were still things Tim and I could do. We created a mold our hands held together dipped in melted Crayola wax; we named and wrapped our very own Crayola crayon; we turned our likenesses into a coloring page; we visited the Guinness World Record biggest crayon named "Big Blue" and so much more. It was a day I will not soon forget. Not to mention the fact that I was able to cross this item off my bucket list.

At the end of the day we went to visit the souvenir shop. Of course, they had everything you could possibly imagine made by Crayola. Tim and I wandered around checking everything out. In the very back of the store was the photo counter where you could pick up your picture that had been taken when you first entered the factory. Even though they were a bit pricey, I still wanted to get one as a keepsake from the day. Unfortunately, as it never seems to fail, they were having issues with their printer. So, while I waited, Tim went to look for the souvenirs we both like to collect; him a pressed penny and me a tack pin.

After several minutes, Tim returned excited to have found his pressed penny. However, he was not able to locate a tack pin for me. This happens sometimes, so when it does I usually get a small magnet or keychain that I can glue onto the corkboards that I have with my tack pin collection on them. My sweetheart informed me that there were a few choices of magnets and keychains, so he would rather I make the decision of what I wanted, while he took my place in line still waiting for that picture.

I meandered around the shop trying to decide what I wanted. I finally settled on a keychain that had the Crayola Factory logo and location on one side and a person's name on the other. I grabbed one off the rounder and took it to show Tim. Sadly, he was a bit unimpressed by my choice and the cost of this item was a bit pricey. We talked about what I wanted to do. Tim suggested that I should just get another pressed penny like his since that would only cost 51 cents versus the $9.99 for the keychain. Not that my husband is cheap but what he said made perfect sense. Since I was going to have to glue whatever I got to my corkboard anyway, it truly would not matter. So, I agreed with him that would be the best way to go.

Tim proposed for me to stay in line to wait for our photo while he would get the pressed penny. After which, he would go get the car and pull it up to the front of the building since it had begun to sleet and rain while we had been in the factory. I agreed to his plan. However, the wait for our picture went on and on, to the point a manager had to come to try to rectify the situation. Once the manager was finally able to print out our photo, he informed me to be sure I came to see him at the checkout counter, so he could give us a discount for our inconvenience. I thanked him for his help and turned to head toward the cashiers.

Now you must understand that there are moments, as I have gotten older, when I forget things. Even those things that were just recently discussed. So, when so much time had passed while I waited to get our picture and with all the confusion that had gone along with that ordeal, I had completely forgotten what Tim and I had decided to do as a replacement for my tack pin. As I headed to the checkout counter and passed the display of named keychains that I had looked at previously, as a substitute for my tack pin, my brain said, "Oh yea, I wanted one of those, as well," and so I just grabbed one off the top row, without even looking at it. It wasn't until I was in line to pay, that suddenly, the fog lifted from my brain and I remembered, "No, silly you had decided not to get the keychain." I didn't want to step out of line and lose my spot to put the keychain back, so I figured I would just hand it over to the manger when I saw him to pay for my other purchases.

While I was going over all that in my head, I flipped the keychain over for the first time and saw the name "Jennifer" staring back at me! I almost dropped everything I was holding from the sudden shock. "Are you kidding me?" From a four-sided rack of probably 40 to 50 names on each side, I pick the one keychain with my daughter's name on it, without even looking. I just couldn't believe it.

By that time, it was my turn to move up and pay at the register where the manager was presiding. I made a quick decision to keep that souvenir and pay for it along with all my other items.

Once outside and in the car with Tim, I quickly explained to him what had just taken place. He was as dumbfounded as I was.

Then, like that wasn't enough of a sign for us, when we got home and out of our vehicle, we walked up to our front steps. Not one, but two dimes laid out on the sidewalk directly in our path. There was no way they had been there when we left in the morning as we would have surely seen them. And yet there they were, staring up at us! What a crazy, crazy day. I can only assume my beautiful daughter wanted us to know she had tagged along and enjoyed the "Crayola Factory" as much as we did.

CHAPTER 14

WHAT DO YOU BELIEVE?

There is an old quote that asserts "Time heals all wounds." However, I do not believe that to be a true statement. Instead I lean more towards a quote made by **Rose Kennedy** that states: "It has been said, 'time heals all wounds.' I do not agree. The wounds remain. In time, the mind, protecting its sanity, covers them with scar tissue and the pain lessens. But it is never gone." Even this quote isn't true all the time for me. There are instances, especially at night, when the pain of losing Jennifer comes rushing back and overwhelms me! The agony of my loss can be so intense that I can barely breathe. It feels like my heart is going to shatter into a million pieces.

Grief is a funny thing. You never know when it is going to overcome you. It might be a street sign; or a commercial; or a television show or a social event; or just something someone says.

A perfect example of this was when a friend of mine from my old school district on Long Island lost her husband. He had been battling cancer for several years. She has put up a lovely post on Facebook how both she and her daughter got to hold their husband / father as he slowly passed from this world into the next. I was sharing this very touching post with my husband when out of nowhere it was like a dam had burst open and the flood gates could no longer hold the water back. I began to cry hysterically. Then from somewhere deep inside, without my even realizing it, I spouted out how I never got to say good-bye to my daughter before she left me! Yes, I had gotten to see her physical body in the hospital after she passed. But that was not the same as a mother holding her child while they were still alive and being able to convey to that child how much they are loved and would be missed. This is a regret I will carry with me to my dying day. I was somewhat aware that this bothered me but not nearly as much as that explosion of emotions made me aware. It is at those moments that I am thankful I have my wonderful husband, Tim, and my treasure trove of dimes.

I am sure that there are still many skeptics out there who believe that the dimes I find are just coincidences or flukes of nature. I can't say I don't blame them. I too have questioned on more occasions than I can count whether or not the dimes truly are signs from my Jen. Sometimes I wonder if I just desire the dimes so badly that it has given me a heightened awareness for finding them. But then I look at all the stories I have just relayed to you in this book. Plus there are so many other examples such as: finding a dime on an abandoned overpass on Rt. 80 in New Jersey; locating several along the riverbank of the Delaware river; stepping on one outside of our hotel room while on vacation in North Carolina; finding one on an abandoned road in the town of Centralia (several different times); even discovering one in the woods while out hiking and so on and so on! With all these examples how can they all be coincidences?

I truly believe that signs and small miracles are all around us if we just open ourselves up to receiving these little gifts from heaven. The gift my daughter chooses to leave me is dimes but for others it might be something else. In the course of writing this book and sharing my story I have had the privilege to hear from others some of their amazing tales, as well.

One such story was from a few years back when I was still working at the schools. The nurse at the time had a daughter-in-law who lost her father suddenly due to a car accident. She told me that the day of the funeral her daughter-in-law and her mother had made a pit stop at a gas station after they had been to the cemetery to bury their father / husband. The daughter-in-law ran into the shop to get something to drink. Supposedly, this girl *never* drank soda but for some unknown reason when she went to the cooler, she was compelled to grab a can of soda instead of her usual bottle of water. It was not until she got back into the car with her mom that they both noticed the can had a name on it. This was an advertising campaign by certain soda companies, at the time. The name on that particular can that the daughter had picked up, was the father's! Now I ask you, why did that wife pick that convenience store to stop at? Why did that daughter choose a can of soda that day instead of water, her usual drink of choice? Why would it be the father's name on the can when there were millions of names it could have been?

More recently, I have a family member who lost her husband suddenly due to a motorcycle accident over Memorial weekend. One day in late August, while she was outside walking the property, she came across the most beautiful pansy she had ever seen. Problem being, pansies are an early spring flower when it is cooler, not a late August bloomer when temperatures had been in the high 80's and 90's. Plus, this particular flower was in a spot where they had never planted any pansies. Her husband's favorite flower? Pansies! So again, I ask. Why a pansy and not some other type of flower? Why right along her footpath by the house? Why at that time of the year?

These types of stories go on and on. From material objects being found that mattered to the deceased; to noticing a sudden lingering smell, like a tobacco scent or a favorite cologne enjoyed by the one who passed; to butterflies and birds acting in a strange fashion such as landing on someone in a special way or by showing up and staying for an extended period of time. I am sure if you were to take a poll between family and friends you would find someone who has some type of similar story to tell. So, what does this all mean?

In the early 1990's there was a television series on the ABC network entitled "Doogie Howser, M.D." starring Neal Patrick Harris as a child prodigy who becomes a doctor at a very young age. In one particular episode entitled "Doogie's Wager," the Doogie Howser character helps deliver a premature baby for a couple who has been trying to conceive a child for twelve years. Since the child arrives three months prematurely, it is placed in a neo-natal unit while it struggles to stay alive. Doogie does everything within his medical powers to help keep the child alive but is frustrated by the fact that with all he is doing, it still may not be enough to save the child. It is at this point that he begins to contemplate the idea of having 'Faith."

While pacing in his bedroom, Doogie absent-mindedly tosses a basketball against a poster of Albert Einstein on the wall. At that very moment Albert seems to come alive and addresses Doogie about his concerns. Doogie explains to Mr. Einstein his dilemma as a scientist and wonders out loud if there is any justification in having 'Faith' and believing in a higher power. Albert Einstein asks Doogie if he has ever heard of "Paschel's Wager." He continues by explaining that Paschel was a French mathematician who was very logical but, he also reasoned that we can never really know for sure if there is a God. However, Paschel goes on to say that it is a good bet to believe in one because we get all the benefits of believing, such as: *life everlasting, personal guidance, enlightenment, evolution;* and *mercy.* Doogie then asks Albert Einstein, "What if God doesn't truly exist?" Mr. Einstein's response is that of Mr. Paschel's which is, "Big deal, you don't lose anything by believing, but look at all you lose if you don't!" At the end of the episode, Doogie writes in his computer journal: "When the tools of science meet the mysteries of faith, the most powerful of all human miracles is born. It is called hope!" I guess that is why my dimes mean so much to me; they are my symbol of hope! Hope in a life everlasting where someday I get to see my daughter once again. Besides, as Mr. Paschel has so poignantly pointed out, what does it hurt to believe?

I just recently saw a post that has been shared and "Liked" on Facebook more than 1,161,014 times.

It is entitled "Pennies from Heaven." It read as follows:

I found a penny today
Just lying on the ground
But it's not just a penny
This little coin I've found
"Found" pennies come from heaven
That's what my Grandpa told me
He said angels toss them down
Oh, how I loved that story
He said when an angel misses you
They toss a penny down
Sometimes just to cheer you up
Make a smile out of your frown
So, don't pass by that penny
When you're feeling blue
It may be a penny from heaven
That an angel tossed to you

By C. Mashburn
Heal Ourselves, Heal the World

With so many "Shares" and "Likes" I can only determine that there are more people than not, who believe the same way I do about the wonderful signs we receive from our departed souls.

For hundreds of thousands of years, mankind has struggled with some type of belief in the afterlife. Science has even gone so far as to try to prove it exists. But in the end, no one truly knows for sure. For a large majority of us, we hold onto that belief that yes, there is a heavenly kingdom after this one, where we will once again be reunited with our loved ones. What does it hurt to believe? I choose to because it gives me the solace I need to wake up and face each new day.

Shortly after Jennifer's death, I had a drinking glass commissioned from her college with the alma mater logo engraved on it. As much as Jennifer loved the high school she attended, she adored the college that she graduated from as well. I thought by having this glass made, it would give me a great container to put all of the dimes that I have found and collected since my daughter's passing. As of today, there are **1724** dimes in that glass. That does not include all the special dimes that have either been glued to something; such as her picture frame at my office; the Jennifer Christmas ornament that Tim and I found; the wooden angel plaque from Tim's mom; the lawyer's business card who got me my divorce and so many other items. In addition, any dimes we have found while out with the car, have been stored in a special compartment in our vehicle. So, there are probably easily close to 2,000 dimes that have been collected in the past seven years. That sheer number, should mean something. Coincidence, I don't think so!

I will state that in the beginning of this ordeal, I did find a tremendous number of dimes, more than I do now. Sometimes, I get frustrated by NOT finding any dimes when I truly want them.

However, it never seems to amaze me that when I am least expecting it or when I am facing a particularly difficult day, that is when my sweet Jennifer will surprise me with one of her tokens of love.

An example being, when Tim and I celebrated our third wedding anniversary. All day I had looked for my sign that my beautiful daughter was blessing our special day but to no avail! Tim planned a wonderful day for us. He took me for a lovely drive with some fun stops along the way but NO dime. We went for a hike around a special lake we truly appreciate but NO dime. Then we finished our day with dinner at a special restaurant but still no dime! It wasn't until after dinner when Tim returned to the car where I was waiting for him that he says to me, "Close your eyes and stick out your hand." Suddenly I felt two small objects fall into my outstretched palm. Opening my eyes, I see two shiny but wet dimes sitting in my hand. Tim informed me that he found them on the floor of the restroom (and thankfully, was thoughtful enough to have washed them!) before placing them into my waiting hand. So sometimes Jennifer sends the dimes directly to me and other times she sends them through a special messenger. Either way, I feel blessed to receive them.

This is why I am sharing my story with all of you. In hopes that my loss and struggles will help someone else who may be dealing with either the same type of situation or something similar. All I do know is that because of my faith and the belief in my signs, I have been able to move forward and carry on. Some days are easier than others, but I still try to make the best of each day when I can. When I can't, I have learned to lean on the goodness and kindness of my family and friends. And if I am really lucky, I may even find a dime to help me get by!

JENNIFER'S DIMES

CONCLUSSION

One of the many things I have learned about grief is that *every* person deals with it differently. When my Jennifer passed, I was attending a church where I knew of a woman who had also lost a daughter in her early twenties. Once things settled down with the funeral and Joe's graduation, I was very anxious to get back to church and speak with her. I was hoping she might be able to share some insight into how I should be dealing with the grieving process. Plus, I thought it would be nice to speak to someone who truly understood what I was going through. However, when I did finally get to speak to her, it was apparent she was not going to be able to help me like I thought. Turns out after three years of her daughter being gone, this mother was still sneaking into the cemetery at night to sit on her daughter's grave, as well as, totally withdrawing from her family at home. Unfortunately, this poor woman was not able to move forward in her grieving process and it was taking a toll on both her younger son and husband. This was when I truly learned that *each* person goes through the grief process at different paces, and some just never move past the loss of their loved one. At least, this woman was willing to go back to church and was trying to find some answers. My wish for her is that someday she will be able to move forward. I, on the other hand, felt the need and the calling to write this book to help with my grieving process. So that is what I have done.

This book was written for the sole purpose of passing along a true-life event that was very traumatic but also eye-opening in ways I never expected. As horrible as losing a child can be, I truly believe if we are open to it, God gives us the strength and means to be able to handle any tragedy. We just have to have "Faith" and be willing to look for God's love and support! By sharing my ordeal with you, my hope is that it will open you up to receiving your own special signs from heavenly forces up above.

I would also like to thank all of my family and friends who have helped me along this difficult journey called "LIFE!" There are days I know I would not have made it through if it wasn't for you. God truly blesses us in ways we never expect. My wish for you is to receive your share of blessings as well. Hopefully, this story has touched you in ways you never thought possible.

If you have been given this book by either someone you may know or by me personally, it is because we thought you may enjoy reading this story. Hopefully, it may even help you if you are dealing with any type of issues in your own personal life, as well.

If after reading this story, you think it would benefit someone you know, please feel free to pass it along to them as well. If you wish to keep your copy but would like another one to pass along to someone, you can either purchase a copy from Amazon or you can contact me directly at the following address:

Barbara L. Acker
PO Box 6
Harleigh, PA 18225

jennifersdimes@yahoo.com

Like us @ Jennifers Dimes on Facebook

Please note: A percentage of the proceeds from the sale of this book will be donated to Molloy College for the "Jennifer Zontini" Scholarship fund. Thank you for your support.

May God truly bless you!

Made in the USA
Columbia, SC
13 September 2018